The Longing of the Heart

The Longing of the Heart

Augustine's Doctrine on Prayer

T.J. van Bavel

PEETERS
LEUVEN – WALPOLE, MA
2009

A CIP record for this book is available from the Library of Congress.

For the original Dutch edition: *Als je hart bidt ... Augustinus' leer over het gebed.* Heverlee-Leuven 2001, Augustijns Historisch Instituut.
The English translation has been reviewed and corrected by D. Foley.

Cover: Augustine (Sculpture by François Demassieux, 1986).

D.2009/0602/105
ISBN 978-90-429-1975-4

**If we lift up our hearts to God,
our hearts are his altar.**

The City of God X, 3, 2 (PL 41, 280)

CONTENTS

Introduction

We do not know Augustine if we do not recognize the praying person in him. He knew how to unite introspection, prayer, intellectual work, and pastoral dedication into a harmonious whole in his daily life. Even though he never wrote a systematic work on the subject of prayer, his personal experiences are related countless times in his writings. His *Confessions*, an accounting of sin and thanksgiving, stand as a monument in history. His *Expositions of the Psalms* were, for him, as a pastor, a select opportunity to appeal to his faithful to live a life of prayer as well. With that, we have indicated the two most significant sources for this book. But even among his other writings or sermons, one finds hardly any in which the topic of prayer is entirely absent. Many of his thoughts have exerted a great influence upon spiritual leaders and guides of more recent ages.

The dialogue with God was the defining element in his life, and he did not hesitate to share his more intimate thoughts with the citizens, merchants, and seafarers of the port cities of Hippo and Carthage. We have good insights into Augustine's internal development. Even as a child, he prayed: "So it came about that even then in boyhood I began to pray to you, my aid and refuge. By calling upon you I untied the knots of my tongue and begged you, in my little-boy way but with no little earnestness, not to let me be beaten at school."[1] Here we have a child's prayer of petition. His life of prayer is far more mature when he is preparing himself for his baptism at Cassiciacum, near Milan. There we find a more definite influence from the psalms and songs he and his companions had heard in the church of Milan. There we hear how he spent an entire night searching for God and reflecting upon the relationship between God and the world.[2] Concerning

[1] Conf. I,9,14.
[2] Ord. 1,3,6-8,22.

the days just prior to his conversion, he writes: "How loudly I cried out to you, my God, as I read the psalms of David, songs full of faith, outbursts of devotion with no room in them for the breath of pride! Uncouth I was in real love for you, a catechumen on holiday in a country house with another catechumen, Alypius; but my mother kept us company, woman in outward form but endowed with virile faith, uniting the serenity of an elderly person with a mother's love and Christian devotion. How loudly I began to cry out to you in those psalms, how I was inflamed by them with love for you".[3] At Cassiciacum, without a doubt, Augustine made great progress in a contemplative attitude toward life. There, he, himself says, he experienced a foretaste of the eternal reality that is so intensely present that sometimes he no longer needed his reasoning understanding.[4]

After Augustine had returned to North Africa, he began to embody his ideal in his parental house in Thagaste: living a contemplative life in seclusion with a small group of like-minded people. It was his goal to become more like God through the practice of asceticism and virtues. The small community strove toward joy, happiness, rest, safety, and intimacy with God. In part, this ideal was still strongly colored philosophically by the Neo-Platonists.[5] Possidius describes Augustine's lifestyle, and that of his followers at Thagaste in a more Christian sense. He writes that Augustine, together with the members of his community, lived for God in fasting, prayer, good works, and in contemplating God's law day and night. The insights that God gave Augustine in prayer and meditation, he shared with his house-mates and other people in oral instruction, or in his writings.[6]

Thus, there can be no doubt that Augustine was, by his very nature, strongly contemplative, but he could realize his ideal only in part, because after just three years, the people invited him to be

[3] Conf. 9,4,8.
[4] Ep. 4,2.
[5] Ep. 10,2.
[6] Vita Augustini 3.

their bishop. Even though we do not know precisely the moment in his life that it occurred, we know that Augustine did consider fleeing into solitude: "Filled with terror by my sins and my load of misery I had been turning over in my mind a plan to flee into solitude, but you forbade me, and strengthened me by your words. *To this end Christ died for all, you reminded me, that they who are alive may live not for themselves, but for him who died for them. See, then, Lord: I cast my care upon you* (2 Cor 5:15) that I may live, and I will contemplate the wonders you have revealed".[7] Fortunately, Augustine remained a man of prayer to the extent that it was possible for him to do so, as bishop. Most of the texts we shall cite in this book date precisely from the time that the monk Augustine also served simultaneously in the office of bishop.

The difficulty in writing this book on prayer according to Augustine lies not in the dearth of material, but rather, in the over-abundance of texts. I have chosen in favor of a systematic exposition of the texts. I believe that this is more convenient for the present day reader. To this end, I have had to split up many texts and categorize the various ideas in their distinctive rubrics. Inevitably, that resulted in repetitions. Here and there, I attempted to circumvent this difficulty by including an index of subjects and names.

Insofar as the scriptural text in Augustine's writings is concerned, I should like to point out that in some instances, it differs markedly from the text that is currently in circulation. This is especially true of the texts from the Old Testament. In addition, the numbering of the palms for Augustine differs from the present day numbering, which conforms to the Hebrew text. Augustine interpreted some palms twice.

[7] Conf. 10,47,70.

I. On the Nature of Prayer

The Reason for Our Prayers

Why is it that people actually pray? Where does the deepest reason for prayer lie? In our daily experiences, we note that in dire situations, people readily begin to pray. This is even found to be true among non-believers. Is this not the case because when in great misery or dire need, humans feel that they are lonely and powerless, and therefore, they turn toward a power that is greater than themselves? The greater power may assume various guises. It may be one's own mother, fate, an impersonal spirit that governs everything, or a personal God. In all religious observances, the prayer of supplication appears to be the one that recurs most frequently. The use of the words "prayer" and "praying" points, indeed, to the primacy of asking in the communication between human beings and God. The deed in which divine worship becomes visible shows us human beings as suppliants. But fortunately, there are many other forms of prayer as well, forms we shall address in detail.

In the Judeo-Christian tradition, prayer is a direct relationship between human beings and a personal God who eternally rules over us. Praying is an activity in which the relationship between the human being and God is experienced and given shape. For us, God is the origin, the most profound reason, and the ultimate goal, not only of ourselves, but of everything that exists. According to Augustine, every human being experiences the fact that he or she is, indeed, leading an independent existence, but that he or she nevertheless belongs to God. No one is sufficient in him- or herself, nor is he or she the ultimate reason for his or her existence. In every life, moments occur in which we experience our own limitations and the fact that we have been created. Augustine phrased it unforgettably in the opening words to his *Confessions:*

> "Great are you, O Lord, and exceedingly worthy of praise; your power is immense, and your wisdom beyond reckoning. And so we humans, who are a tiny part of your creation, long to praise you, we who carry our mortality about with us, carry the evidence of our sin and with it the proof that you thwart the proud. Yet these humans, tiny part of your creation as they are, still do long to praise you. You arouse us so that praising you may bring us joy, because you have made us and drawn us to yourself, and our heart is unquiet until it rests in you".[1]

In this text, two thoughts come sharply to the fore. The first is that of the sinfulness and hubris of human beings who believe they are sufficient in and of themselves. Whoever believes they do not need God will be destroyed by their own weakness and sinfulness. Whoever relies solely upon him- or herself will come to an end in him- or herself as well. It is precisely the recognition of God that leads us to break out from our own ego. Our finite nature is broken through; it is broken open to the Infinite. The second thought is immediately linked to this, namely that of "being created in your image" (Gen. 1,26-27). The words "in your image" express the fact that we were created as the "charter" or rather, as the "original message" of our humanity. It would be wrong, however, to envisage our created-ness as a fact relating to a remote past and nothing more. No, the idea denotes life and movement. As creatures, human beings are en route to God as their most ultimate future. Dependence from God must be translated into attachment to God. Our origin wants to be also our future. The restlessness of the human heart is thus borne up by two motives: consciousness of our weakness or sinfulness, and the conviction that we are merely created beings, negligible particles within the whole of God's creation. The rest that we hope to find in God therefore signifies the abdition both of our moral imperfection and of our mortality.

The fact that God is the creator of all means that he encompasses and contains everything. In this regard, Augustine makes

[1] Conf. I,1,1. See also En. Ps. 55,17.

repeated reference to Romans 11:36 *From him, through him, and in him are all things.* He fills heaven and earth. "If I ascend to heaven, there you sit; if I fall down into the underworld, God is present there also" (Ps. 139: 8). God is spiritually present in created reality, but in a manner that is wonderful and hardly to be comprehended.[2] With these last words, Augustine wishes to stress that God does, indeed, encompass the whole of creation, but that the reverse is not the case: creation does not encompass God. God remains greater and more than the created things. He casts a sharp light on this in his *Confessions:*

> "Or should I say, rather, that I should not exist if I were not in you, from whom are all things, through whom are all things, in whom are all things?... Are you not everywhere in your whole being, while there is nothing whatever that can hold you entirely?"[3]

Thus, God's majesty makes him present in all beings, while at the same time, he surpasses them. Here we are dealing with the deeply religious topic of God who is at once close by, and yet far removed. His presence in his creation puts him close at hand, but his unfathomable light puts him at an infinite distance. Creation does not exhaust God's possibilities, and for that reason, the human heart remains restless until it finds rest in God.

In addition, God is not present in all creatures in the same way. His presence in things, in nature, in plants and animals, is different from his presence in human beings. The believer in God the Creator finds traces of God in nature, that is to say, things that human beings can bring to the search for God. But in an entirely distinctive way God is present in human beings, because they are created in God's image. Unlike the other creatures, human beings possess understanding that causes them to reflect and gives them insight, and a free will that enables them to receive and to give love. In this we are, according to Augustine, an image of God. In our hearts, in our deepest being, we carry this image which cannot

[2] En. Ps. 81,2.
[3] Conf. I,2,2-3,3. See also En. Ps. 5,2.

be destroyed. We may darken or mutilate the image of God that is within us, but we cannot eradicate it. The fact that we carry God's image is a powerful appeal to give ourselves back to God. Augustine compares this to the image of the emperor on a coin according to the words of Jesus in Matthew 22:21: Render to Caesar what is Caesar's and to God what is God's. If we bear God's image, we are God's.[4] We belong to God, but not all human beings will recognize that immediately. That is why the faithful can say:

> "Their God, our God? But is there anyone of whom he is not God? No one. Obviously he is not God of everyone in the same way. He is more truly ours, ours because we live on him as on our daily bread...Let the soul say in complete confidence: You are my God, for he says to our soul: I am your salvation (Ps. 35,3)".[5]

Everything that has been said thus far deals with our sinfulness, our limited nature, our status as creatures. God's presence and God's absence constitute for us, as believers, the basis of our prayers. Thus we come into contact with God as the deepest foundation of our existence. Here, entering into contact means that we enter into a relationship with God because he was the first to enter into a relationship with us. This relationship is played out, in the first instance, in our spirit, and it takes shape in a "turning of our hearts toward God".[6] That is an initial, quite general description of prayer. A second description is that prayer is an external or internal talk with God. For this reason, Augustine will describe praying as "speaking to God"[7]. The words "to God" reflect, above all, the direction and movement of our prayer, viewed from the human side. Elsewhere, he describes it as "talking with God.". This expresses more strongly that praying is an inner conversation (*colloquium*) or dialogue. This presupposes that our hearts stand open to God's presence by virtue of the love of God

[4] En. Ps. 4,9.
[5] En. 2 Ps. 32, s. 2,17.
[6] S. Dom. m. II,3,14.
[7] En.Ps. 85,7.

given to our hearts by the Holy Spirit (Romans 5:5). Such a conversation is based upon the fact that God has already given himself to our hearts.[8]

A dialogue or encounter requires, of necessity, two persons. No one would say: I met a stone or a bush. A dialogue or an encounter presupposes consciousness and understanding on both sides. A human being can experience his or her shortcomings and misery, but not know to whom to turn. He or she seeks a sounding board. Whoever believes in God always has a loving sounding board. But, in the case of prayer, there is more is than a sounding board. A crucial aspect is that in praying, the initiative lies with God. God has created us out of love; he was the first one to love us. God expects of us a response to his love. He sought us out before we sought him.[9] We might say that God is waiting for us. But God does not wait in the same way people wait. In most cases, peple are powerless when they wait for something, for instance, when they wait for a bus or a train, for good weather or rain, for a response from someone, for friendship. If we had the power to make things happen ourselves, we would not need to wait for them. God's waiting, on the other hand, has power. It means help for human beings. Thus, for Augustine, God's waiting is characteristic of his patience. In Romans 2:4, Paul represents goodness, patience, and forbearance as the riches of God. In the Scriptures, we find a great number of texts that speak of God's forbearance with the sinner so that the latter might convert. Thus, God's word gives the sinner hope once more. God also expects his vineyard to bear fruit, especially, that human beings honor him, serve him, and love him. Over that he rejoices.[10]

God is first in speaking to us in all sorts of ways. We shall return to the various ways later. But for now, we can present a few general thoughts of Augustine. God himself teaches us to

[8] En. Ps. 4,2.
[9] En. Ps. 69,6.
[10] S. 87,1,1. S. 343,10. S. 145,5. En. Ps. 144,11.

pray. He takes the initiative to the dialogue. It is his voice that sounds in the most intimate reaches of our hearts. Human beings can, indeed, convey God's message, but "He who speaks in us and whom we have received in our hearts, and whose temples we have become, is our best teacher," better than human beings can ever be.[11] The voices of human beings are not insignificant, but they are "transitory stages", one might say, and they sound from afar. They borrow their significance from God himself:

> "O God, my merci, who made me and did not forget me when I forgot you. Into my soul I call you[12]...who before ever I called you into me, called me forestalled me by your persistent, urgent entreaties, multiplying and varying your appeals that I might hear from afar, and turn back, and begin to call you into me who were calling me".[13]

In human beings, thus, we listen to the voice of God. Those proclaimers of the faith who have gone before us interpret the summons from God. In word and deed, they encourage us to turn to God himself. In the process, Augustine compares the itinerant proclaimers of the faith with "precious feet," an image he borrows from Isaiah 52,7: "How welcome in the mountains are the feet of the messenger whose message is peace."

"The Lord is merciful, he is just, and he will be compassionate. In the first place he is merciful, for he bowed down his ear to me. I would never have known how close God's ear was to my mouth had I not been aroused by those beautiful feet (of the preachers) to call him into me; for who has ever called him into his or her heart without firstly being called by him?"[14]

Indeed, we cannot appeal to God if we are not first summoned by him. Thus we are summoned as a Church, to be a part of God's heritage, and Augustine can say: "Being summoned, she

[11] S. 293,1.

[12] See chapter 2: Invoking God.

[13] Conf. 13,1,1.

[14] En. Ps. 114,5.

appeals to God".[15] Although we can thus learn how to pray from others, and we frequently pray with the words of others (just think of the Psalms), it is nevertheless necessary that they become our own words. It is all right to pray with the mouth of another, but we must learn to call out to God with our own mouths. We should, in our prayer, draw on what God has given us, from the inspiration that he gives us.[16] Ultimately, everything comes from God, both the prayers of others as well as our own prayers. No one can say: "I have given God my faith and my prayers". Augustine finds such an attitude to run counter to Paul's text: "Who can demand payment for something that he has given to God?" (Romans 11,35). We can give God nothing that he did not give us first. What we can give God is merely something we have "found;" it was there long before we were able to give it back. Thus, we give God that which is from God, and he receives from us that which he gave us himself. That applies to our faith as well as to our prayers.[17] Therefore, God seeks us through his gifts, but in these gifts, God wants to give himself. He wants to possess us forever. Augustine also describes praying as "the seeking of God's name." This corresponds completely to the fact that God seeks our names, because he wants our names to stand written in heaven forever We have a name there if we do not neglect the name of the Lord. "For if you seek the name of God, God will seek your name."[18]

The Many Ways in which God Speaks to Us

In succession, we want to indicate the ways in which God speaks to us in creation, in and through human beings, through the Holy Scriptures, and through his Word who became a human being, Jesus.

[15] En. Ps. 5,2.
[16] En. Ps. 65,21.
[17] S. 168,5,5.
[18] En. Ps. 91,3.

a) *God Speaks in Creation*

Prior to his conversion, Augustine was, for a number of years, an adherent of Manicheism. From a negative experience of the world, with all its sorrows and miseries, the adherents of Manicheism were firmly convinced that the material world was brought forth by an evil power, and not by a good God. How can anything that is so bad, so transitory, and so imperfect as this world, come from a just and loving God? This world means nothing more than banishment to us. Augustine describes his situation at the time as follows: "They are not in their senses, they, for whom something is displeasing in your creation, any more than I was in my senses when a great number of things that were created by you did not please me."[19]

Augustine's conversion signified a far-reaching change of attitude with respect to the world. We see him immediately take upon himself the defense of the goodness and beauty of creation, because the one and true God of the Bible wanted the world, and created it, and not some evil force other than God. On the other hand, he maintains, with respect to some philosophers of his day, that God does not coincide with the world, or that the world is a part of God. No. God stands above creation, but he remains caring for it because it sprang forth from his goodness. Creation is a gift from God, and for that reason, it is good and beautiful. The love of God precedes creation, and thus it precedes us, too, and remains incomprehensible. Precisely on the basis of his love, God willed nothing but good things, and he hates nothing that he created.[20]

Time after time, in his works, Augustine sings the praises of the goodness and beauty of creation. He praises the goodness of material things, of the body, with its health and fruitfulness in procreation, the beauty of the innards of a lowly animal, of the feather of a bird, of a lowly meadow flower, of the leaf of a tree. Nothing in creation may be rejected.[21]

[19] Conf. VII,14,20.
[20] Io. Eu. tr. 110,6.
[21] Ciu. 7,11.

> "Behold the manyfold and varied beauty of heaven and earth and sea, the abundance and marvellous quality of light, sun and moon and stars, shady woods, the colours and odours of flowers, the many kinds of birds who sing and display their bright-coloured plumage, the diverse kinds of so many animals of all sizes – and the smallest are most admired... Behold also the grandiose spectacle of the sea, when it clothes itself with varied colours as with garments, and sometimes is green, and that too with many variations, sometimes is crimson, sometimes is blue. And what a magnificent sight it is also whenever it is raised by a storm".[22]

The beauty and goodness of that which has been created are not an ultimate goal for Augustine. They raise the question: where does all this come from? Who is the maker of it? Thus, it is a matter of ascending from visible creation to the invisible creator. The acceptance of the invisible creator can only be accomplished by faith. In the process, the eyes of our hearts are as windows through which we look at God's creation.[23] When we are ready to ascribe the whole of creation to God as its maker, it becomes, so to speak, a great book about the nature of things, in which we can read. Naturally, not all the mysteries are then resolved; there will always be things that remain hidden from us.[24] Once we believe in God as the creator of all things, we can call out: if creation is so great and beautiful, how great and beautiful, then, must God be! Thus, earthly beauty is a preparation for the longing for God. The earthly things that we love prompt us to long for God all the more.[25]

> "Let your mind roam round the whole creation. From all sides creation will cry to you: God made me. Whatever delights you in art points you to the artist, and all the more so if you go round the whole created order. Gazing on it fills you with longing to praise its maker. You see the heavens: they are the mighty words of God. You

[22] See the whole passage in ciu. 22,24,1-5.

[23] S. 126,2,3.

[24] C. Faust. 32,20.

[25] En. Ps. 84,9.

> see the earth: God made the numbers of different seeds, the different species of plants, the great multitude of animals...Everything everywhere calls out to you the name of the creator, and the varied beauties of created things are a chorus of praise to him. But who can unravel all the secrets of creation? Who can turn it all into words of praise?... Who could praise as it deserves this force which pulses in us, enlivening the body, moving the limbs, activating the senses, embracing so many things in the memory, sifting out so many by the understanding; who can worthily praise that?"[26]

Some expressions from this passage deserve our attention. The words "calls out to you" and "the beautiful forms are, so to speak, voices that praise" point to the fact that the creatures are, in fact, merely a reflection of the creator and they cannot, in the strictest sense, praise him. Praising is a conscious human action. The irrational creatures need us – if I may express it in this way – to praise God. Through us, they praise God. If the whole of creation calls out through its beauty, then it calls through us, through our contemplation of it, and through our voice.[27] We must admire the splendor of this world, stand humbled in its presence, and praise it, but, from there, we must climb up to God himself.[28]

"Your whole creation never wearies of praising you, never falls silent. Never a breath from the mouth of one who turns to you but gives you glory. Never is praise lacking from the universe of living creatures and material beings as they laud you through the mouths of those who contemplate them. Supported by the things you have made let the human soul rise above its weariness and pass through these creatures to you, who have made them so wonderfully".[29]

The fact that we must lift ourselves to God out of our lethargy is an allusion to the ambiguous role creation can play. We experience the beauty and the power of attraction of the things that

[26] En. 2 Ps. 26,12.
[27] En. Ps. 148,15.
[28] En. Ps. 41,7.
[29] Conf. V,1,1.

have been created, but we can also become entangled in them, so that we no longer think of God. Instead of being a springboard to God they can require all our attention and cause us to forget God. For that reason, Augustine will always stress the fact that the created things are limited and transitory. They can give no firm and ultimate happiness. In this respect, they can also be a source of disillusionment. Augustine experienced the disillusionment himself. The entire account of his conversion is an account of human impotence and of dissatisfaction brought about by the things of this world. He did not hesitate to preach about his experience:

> "Everywhere you find things to love and things to praise. Yes, but how much more worthy of praise is he who made these things which evoke your praise? You have lived under their spell for too long, buffeted by conflicting desires. You bear the marks of the wounds they have dealt you. You are turn apart by these many loves, restless everywhere and nowhere at peace. Gather yourself together into your real self. If anything outside you has been giving you joy, ask who is its author".[30]

By virtue of the fact that nothing created can totally satisfy the urgings of our hearts, our restlessness is aroused. Human beings must slowly gain awareness of their hunger for something higher. "Creation appears to everyone in the same way; but for this one, it remains silent, for that one, it speaks. Or rather: it speaks to all, but only those understand creation who have tested its voice internally, against the touchstone of truth."[31] Only after our inner eyes have been opened by faith does that which is created assume an entirely positive role. Then creation is, entirely, a comprehensible address from God. Then it is re-shaped to praise of God; then it becomes a revelation of goodness and beauty, in spite of the shadow side that descends upon it due to its being transitory, finite, and limited. Then it becomes one of the many ways in which God seeks to approach us:

[30] En. Ps. 145,5.
[31] Conf. X,6,10.

> "We perceive that each creature has its own origin and source, its own generative power, its due time of birth, its way of maintaining itself, and its decline into death...And in all these there is an invisible something, called spirit or soul. In all living things there is a certain trace of unity which prompts them to seek pleasure, flee from harm, and keep themselves whole...In all this consideration of created beings...let the soul question itself: Who made all these things? Who created them? Who created you, my soul, as one among them all? What are these things you are contemplating? And what are you, who contemplate? Who is he, who made both the things you contemplate, and you, who contemplate them? Who is he?...As you become like him, you draw very near...Consider how the Lord wants us to come close to him. He begins by making us like himself, so that we may come close to him".[32]

This text is a summons to love. Our likeness to God keeps pace with our growth in love, especially in love for our neighbors, and in particular, for our enemies. Thus, creation leads us not only to the worshipful praise of God, but also to love for God, and, by way of that love, to love of one's neighbor. Thus, in the creation, we must see an appeal from God, an encouragement to ascend to him, to praise him, and to love him. "Heaven and earth, and all that they contain, tell me from all sides that I must love you".[33]

b) God Speaks to Us through Human Beings

Who has never been impressed by an encounter with a noble human being? Augustine met many in his career. The account of his conversion is, at the same time, an account of encounters. He experienced these encounters as signs of a sort, signs of God's presence. In them, he was also able to heed God's voice. In addition, a great number of those whom he met were examples to him, models he could follow. In his *Confessions*, he says: "We carried your words with us, bored deep within our hearts, and also the examples of your servants, whom you have made from a darkly glimmering

[32] En. Ps. 99,5.
[33] Conf. 10,6,8.

light, and whom you have made to live from death…set us brightly ablaze".[34] Thus, there is the meeting with the famous ancient physician Vindicianus, who tried to dissuade Augustine from his belief in horoscopes. Augustine came into his confidence, and he was impressed by the lively nature of the man's thoughts. Concerning the meeting, he writes: "Were you, God, not with me, even through the old man? Are you not, through him, going to save my soul?" Vindicianus, together with Augustine's friend, Nebridius, had an admirable soul *(mirabilis animae)*, ensuring that Augustine had given up his belief in astrology.[35] Augustine even knew enough to draw a lesson from the meeting with the Manichean Faustus, and to value Faustus' positive characteristics. The man was so modest that he readily admitted his ignorance in many matters, and thus, Augustine says: "That was reason enough for me to find him a sympathetic figure, because there is more beauty in the modesty of someone who makes such a confession than in the things that I demanded to know".[36] We also know what a great role Simplicianus played in Augustine's conversion. Concerning him, Augustine says: "And you gave me the thought… that I had to turn to Simplicianus. The impression this man made upon me was that of a good servant to you, and your grace shown within him." Simplicianus told Augustine the story – a story that afforded an outstanding opportunity to accompany the praise of your grace – of the conversion of the famous philosopher Victorinus. It set Augustine aflame to follow Victorinus.[37] A countryman of Augustine's, Ponticianus, who held a high position in the palace at Milan, told of the Egyptian monk, Antonius, of whom Augustine and Alypius had never heard anything at that time. Ponticianus also focused their attention on the communities in the monasteries, and the way in which they lived, not only in the Egyptian desert, but also in a monastery outside the walls of

[34] Conf. 9,2,3.
[35] Conf. 4,3,5 and 7,6,8.
[36] Conf. 5,7,12.
[37] Conf. 8,1,1-2,5 and 5,10.

Milan. He also told how in Treves, two imperial inspectors, friends of his, had given up their posts in order to live an ascetic life as monks. During the narration, so Augustine writes, God was busy "snatching them from behind his back and placing them before his own eyes," that is to say: God made him see who he in fact was and gave him a deeper understanding of himself.[38]

It is sufficiently well-known how much Augustine owed his most trusted friend, Alypius. He called him "the brother of his heart." He was also his companion in conversion and baptism, together with Augustine's son, Adeodatus. Augustine admired Alypius' constant fidelity, his purity of soul, "an unsurpassed master of his body, who could withstand treading on the chill Italian ground in his bare feet with uncommon pluck."[39] The strength with which God spoke to Augustine through his mother, Monnica, hardly needs to be stressed. He drank in the name of Christ, which he could never forget thereafter, with her mother's milk. The simple, yet firm faith of his mother accompanied him throughout his life. The most beautiful praise that he gave her can probably be found in the following words: "Every one of them who knew her extolled and honored and loved you, God, highly in her, because everyone became aware of your presence in her heart by the witness that the fruits of her holy life's journey bore."[40]

In these examples – and there are, without doubt, many more that could be found in his works – Augustine heard the voice of God. They were for him a reminder and an impetus to turn toward God and to praise God in these human beings. In his journey toward God, the lament did escape him: "I was, without doubt, still far removed from the spiritual greatness of these human beings."[41] But is this not a sign of the fact that human beings give each other life, even spiritual life? In meeting with

[38] Conf. 8,6,14-7,16.
[39] Conf. 9,6,14.
[40] Conf. 9,9,22.
[41] Conf. 6,12,21.

good and noble human beings, we come into contact with important values which we, ourselves, might not yet be able to embody, but they glow before us, like a light. People give each other light, beauty, and goodness, and all these values are radiations from God. "For with you God, lives that which is good for us, without ever diminishing, and that good is you, yourself."[42] In this life, in any case, God works in and through us.[43]

c) God Speaks to Us in the Holy Scriptures

The book of nature is not the principal book by means of which God addresses the human heart. Not even human beings who make God's voice speak for us play the primary role because, ultimately, they borrow their words from the Word of God, as revealed to us by the Holy Scriptures. Thus, in the final analysis, Augustine's conversion is attributable to the Holy Scriptures, however much people have helped him in the process. The place of the Holy Scriptures in Augustine's life as a Christian is something we could not emphasize enough. His primary concern was to study and consider the Scriptures, and constantly to make progress in them. There he sought the reason and inspiration for his mode of living, his spirituality, his contemplation, and his theology. He writes: "Let your Scriptures be my delight…your voice is my joy". He calls upon his believers to follow him: "We must make a nest in our hearts for the Word of God."[44]

First, God speaks to us, and then we speak to God. Prayer is thus no monologue. God's words – in fact the whole of the Holy Scriptures – come first. Thus, Augustine's description of praying:

> "Your prayer is a conversation with God. When you read, God is speaking to you. When you pray, you are speaking to God".[45]

[42] Conf. 4,16,31.
[43] Conf. 13,37,52.
[44] Conf. 11,2,3. S. 343,1.
[45] En. Ps. 85,7.

"Reading" is clearly taken here to mean reading the Holy Scriptures. The same thought comes to the fore at other places:

> "Let God speak to us in the readings, let us speak to God in our prayers. If we listen obediently to his words, then the one we pray to is dwelling in us".[46]

> "Pray what you hear, and pray while you listen".[47]

This thought also applies to the words with which Jesus proclaimed his joyful message to us. None of us hears him still speaking in the way in which he spoke to the throng in Palestine. We hear him speaking only in the Holy Scriptures and in his servants, who pass the words of the Scriptures on to us. In the readings and the homilies during each liturgical celebration, we still hear his voice today.[48] But the word of God, or of Jesus is not something that remains noncommittal. It is not something that we can fashion to our own taste. It is something new; it penetrates within our being and breaks us open. It demands a great deal, because it always signifies a call to live according to the Word. It is a call to turn around, to change one's life, or at least, to strive for the better.

> "Truth, you respond clearly, but not all hear you clearly. They all appeal to you about what they want, but do not always hear what they want to hear. Your best servant is the one who is less intent on hearing from you what accords with his own will, and more on embracing with his will what he has heard from you".[49]

The words "embracing what one hears from God" instruct us to carry out what we hear in the concrete life of every day. They point the way toward living God's law: "If you want your prayers to be fixed in God's ear, fix his law in your hearts".[50] But maintaining God's law is a gradual process. It progresses from virtue to virtue:

[46] S. 219.
[47] En. Ps. 42,4.
[48] S. 17,3,3.
[49] Conf.10,26,37.
[50] En. Ps. 85,10.

> "Grace will come after the law, and grace is itself a blessing. And what does this grace and this blessing grant us? That we will walk from many powers (= moral virtues) to one single power (= Christ) (1 Cor. 1:24)...But now it is still a time of prayer and petition and sometimes of some rejoicing, though only in hope".[51]

For this reason, the Word of God has a healing and purifying power. It liberates us from the wrong paths; it frees us whenever we are entangled in ourselves.[52] It puts us face to face with ourselves and reveals our shortcomings and failures to us. Augustine finds a clear example of that in David's life. The word that the prophet Nathan speaks out in the name of God allows David to see what he has actually done by allowing Uriah to be killed in order to take his wife.[53] Augustine uses the same words here as those in which he describes his own conversion: my sin, which was behind me, is now placed before me.[54] But if the word of God possesses a purifying power, prayer possesses it as well, for prayer is entering into a dialogue with God's word. The intention of our prayers renders our hearts serene and purifies them; it renders the heart more suitable to receive Godly gifts. [55]

And yet, God's Word plays more than a healing role. It also has the role of revealing God's love to us. Taking the image of the "arrow" as a point of departure, Augustine will describe God's words as arrows of love. "You have transfixed our hearts with the arrow of your love, and we bear your words within us, attached to our inmost recesses".[56] We find the same idea in the following text: "You have hit my heart with your words, and I have begun to love you.".[57] In a sermon, he clarifies what he means by the arrows. In one interpretation of the words "The sharp arrows of the mighty" (Psalm 120:4) he says:

51 En. Ps. 83, 11-12.
52 En. 3 Ps. 36, 12.
53 En. Ps. 50,8.
54 See also En. Ps. 143,6.
55 S. Dom. m. 2,3,14.
56 Conf. 9,2,3.
57 Conf. 10,6,8.

> "Sharp arrows of the mighty one are the words of God. Watch them when they are launched and see how they pierce hearts. But when human hearts are transftxed by the arrows of God's word, the effect is not death but the arrousal of love. The Lord is a skilled marksman with his eye on love. No one shoots more beautiful arrows of love than with words. Such a person shoots at the heart of the lover for the good of the lover. He shoots to turn you into his lover. Each time we perform something with words, it is like with arrows".[58]

God's sharp, most powerful arrows have, in most cases, the purpose of bringing us to love of God once God has rendered his love knowable to us. Augustine pointed directly to the Song of Songs, 2:5 and 5:8 "For I am wounded by love," words by which the bride expresses her fiery longing for the bridegroom.[59] Of course, the healing role of God's arrows is not excluded altogether. Sometimes God's sharp arrows are commandments or orders that strike the hearer's heart in a painful way.[60] God's words can also be reproachful or threatening words. Because God has entrusted his words to his servants, it is obvious that their words, too, are described as the arrows of God. Thus, the martyrs slung God's arrows into the faces of their persecutors, that is to say, they hit them with the divine word.[61] Even the Evangelists and the Apostles are, for Augustine, arrows in the hand of the Almighty. And if there are any Christians who still feel no love for the Apostles, let them feel the arrow of the Apostles' words in their hearts, for the wound of love is salutary.[62]

[58] En. Ps. 119, 5.
[59] En. Ps. 44,16.
[60] En. Ps. 143,13.
[61] En. Ps. 39,16.
[62] En. Ps. 17,15. En. Ps. 126,11. S. 298,2,2.

II. Praying as Being in God's Presence

1. Invoking God

One of the most significant expressions of prayer is appealing to God. That is the usual way in which we translate the Latin word *invocatio.* But Augustine always gives preference to a literal interpretation of the word: calling in, or calling God into, that is to say, calling God into one's own heart. For him, "to call to" is too weak. In the expression "call to someone," the emphasis is placed upon the distance that lies between the one who calls and the one being called. Just consider the following example: if we call to someone in the street, we do so to attract the other person's attention, the person who appears to be walking past unaware of us. It is a different matter if we call someone into our home or within us; in the sense of inviting a person, this is much more intimate.

Prayer is a matter of a personal relationship to God. If we seek God for his own sake, we know that his attention is always directed toward us. When Augustine interprets the text "The unrighteous who do not call God within and quake out of fear where there was no fear" (Psalm 13:5), he expressly states: "They did not call God into themselves. They did not invite the Lord into their hearts. They did not wish to be the dwelling-place of the Lord".[1] To seek God for his own sake has particular meaning for Augustine. There are people who are eager for God's gifts, but not for God himself. But in that case, one remains far removed from a personal relationship. The same applies to human relationships. If we regard someone for the sake of his or her gifts, we never achieve the depth of love, for the beloved seeks to be loved for his or her own sake, as a person. The person, him- or herself is of value to someone who loves.

[1] En. Ps. 76,2.

> "Many call upon God, but they do not invoke God. To invoke God is to call God into yourself, for this is what "invocatio" means: to call him in. But you would not presume to invite a person of such authority into your home, unless you know how to prepare a fit place in which to entertain him".[2]

Invoking thus has everything to do with love. No one wants to accord in things to him- or herself that he or she holds in no regard. Everyone opens him- or herself only to those things or people that are loved.

"You invoke whatever you love. You invoke whatever you call into yourself, you invoke what you want to come to you. Now, if your motive in calling upon God is that money may come to you, or an inheritance come to you, or worldly rank come to you, you are invoking or calling into yourself, the things you want to come to you. But you are making God the accomplice of your greed, not the hearer of your desires... Invoke God as God, love God as God. Nothing is better than he is, so desire God himself, hunger for God".[3]

Whoever loves longs for the beloved. Longing is an aspect of love. And in the loving relationship between two people, longing is reciprocal. Where God is concerned, we must even say that he, himself, gave us this longing.

"Into my soul I call you, for you prepare it to be your dwelling by the desire you inspire in it".[4]

Thus, invoking God is offering one's own heart as a dwelling place for God. Concerning the text "To the Lord I pray: You are my God" (Psalm 140:7), Augustine states that there is no one for whom he is not the true God. God is everyone's God. But in a much stronger way, he is the God of those who enjoy him, who serve him, and are eager to submit to him.[5] The Bishop of Hippo says: "Be God's house and he will be your house. He will dwell in

[2] En. 2 Ps. 30, s.3,4.
[3] En. Ps. 85,8.
[4] Conf. 13,1,1.
[5] En. Ps. 139,10.

you, and you in him," and: "God himself dwells in his own people and they are his dwelling place".[6] Offering one's own heart as a dwelling place seems like an act that seems to come purely from us. It can arouse the impression that we play the major role in praying and that everything depends upon us, but that is not so. God retains the initiative, because he is greater than our hearts. The most important thing remains that we be occupied by God. There is clearly a "passive" or receiving aspect that must be recognised, one that Augustine describes as "being occupied." It is also possible to express it in this way: It is not we who receive the guest who are most important, but the guest himself. This is expressed strongly whenever Augustine goes into deeper detail with respect to Isaiah's prayer, 26:13 "Lord, take possession of us" (the text, as it is found in the Septuagint translation of the Bible).

> "What can we vow to God, except to be God's temple? We can offer nothing more pleasing to him than the prayer found in Isaiah: Take possession of us. In the transference of earthly properties a householder gains something when he acquires rights of ownership, but with the church it is different. The property itself gains by being possessed by such a sublime owner".[7]

Here the Church refers to the communion of believers in its entirety. What occurs in the relationship between the faithful and God stands in contrast to what occurs in the world. There, a person becomes richer by obtaining more worldly possessions. The possessor becomes better off as a result, but not the possession itself. Things are altogether different in the relationship between God and the faithful human being. If we are God's possessions, then we, ourselves become better as a result, and we are enriched. God does not need us to be happy or rich himself, but he wants to possess us in order to make us happy. God wants us to possess him, and he wants to possess us because this extends the advantage to us. "May he possess you so that you might possess him. You shall be his domain, you shall be his house. He possesses you

[6] En. 2 Ps. 30, s.3,8. S. 337,3,3.
[7] En. Ps. 131,3.

for your own advantage. You possess him for your own advantage".[8] "Possessing" has two meanings here: Possessing God, already in this life, and possessing him after this life. Our possession of God on earth is still imperfect, because it consists, particularly, in the spiritual movements of longing, and in the sweetness of hope. Both cases involve a receiving possession.

In this context, Augustine also plays with two meanings of the word "cultus." Cultus means both "Serving God or honoring God" as well as "working a piece of land, or cultivating it." We are, as it were, the Lord's acre. But he can only care for us and work us if we wish to be his acre. If we serve God, he grants us a service and makes us, his acre, fruitful. In short: if God possesses us, it benefits us (as his possession). That is the reciprocal significance of the position: we possess God and he possesses us.[9]

God showed he wanted to possess us by redeeming us by means of his son's blood. Precisely by redeeming us, God made us his dwelling place and temple.[10] Once again, it holds true that we possess God in quite a different manner from the one in which we possess earthly goods. Earthly goods are all of a transitory nature, but God remains eternal. Job is Augustine's great example here. Job lost all that he possessed in terms of temporal goods given by God, but in all his misery, he did not lose God. He remained conscious of the fact that he himself was a possession of God's. He was possessed only by the Lord, and not by earthly goods.[11] With the prayer "Lord, take possession of us" we also gain a prospect on eternity, because the eternal God wants to be our future:

> "Sisters and brothers, was I wrong to say that God will be our property? Suppose; I put it a little differently and say that God will be our inheritance? God, you are my hope, my portion in the land of the living (Ps. 142:6). You, Lord, will be my portion. It is true,

[8] En. Ps. 34,1,12.
[9] En. 2 Ps. 32, s.2,17-18. En. Ps. 134,16.
[10] S. 278,7,7.
[11] S. 21,9.

brothers and sisters, you will be both possessed and possessors. You will be God's possession and God will be your possession by serving him... He will be our possession so that he may feed and tend us, and we shall be his possession so that he may rule us".[12]

2. Prayer as Purification

A pure heart will make us pray. If we invoke God and want Him to come into us, we must purify our hearts[13]. Otherwise, he whom we invite cannot enter.[14]

"Now when you invoke God, you call or invite him into yourself. How do you expect him to come to you, if you have not cleaned up the place you are to receive him in? You are not capable, you say, of clearing up the mess you have made of yourself. Call him to clean it up, invite him in to help you to do it".[15]

Invoking is a matter of love. Every human being invokes only what or whom he or she loves. Things or people that are held in no regard will not be welcomed into one's presence, as we have already seen. But if we invite God within us, the dwelling place of God, which is ourselves, must be in good order as well. There must be room for God, and there must be nothing that prevents him from coming in. In other words: there must be nothing that is in contradiction with God. And what is in greater conflict with God than sin? Sin consists in a lack of love for God. Sin and God constitute an internal contradiction. For that reason, there may be no unjust chase after profits, no lust for fame, no blasphemy, no adultery, no deception, or evil longing in a person's heart. If there is, there is no room for God.

"What you are invoking is money, not God. You cannot get the money you covet... so you call God in to help. By making God

[12] En. Ps. 145,11.
[13] En. 2 Ps. 33,8.
[14] En. 2 Ps. 30, s.3,8.
[15] S. 47,7,8.

the agent of your enrichment, you have made God the errand boy of yourself. Do you really want to invoke God? Then invoke him for nothing else but himself... How can you find satisfaction in the things God has made, if God himself does not satisfy you?".[16]

Purifying our hearts applies not only to grievous sins. It also applies with respect to our attachment to earthly goods, however good they may be in their own right, such as health, a successful marriage, prosperity, a secure financial position, etc. If, in the process, we forget that they are God's gifts, and if we do not love God in all these good things, then, in truth, we do not call God within us.[17] A pure love loves the person for his or her own sake. That is also true of human relationships. If one loves a person solely for considerations of expediency, for example, for the sake of his or her capacities or his or her external appearance, that is, actually, an insult. A human being wants to be loved because of what he or she is, as a person. From this everyday experience, we must state that there is no such thing as pure love directed toward God if our priority is his gifts, rather than himself. The highest gift that a human being or God can give is him- or herself.

3. Praying as Presence

From the previous texts, we can conclude that God wants to possess us and that we must invite God to come into our hearts. We ask that God, who encompasses all things will want to remain in us. These are formulations that make it evident to us that prayer consists in a reciprocal presence: He within me, I within him.

We can easily understand what true presence is from examples drawn from daily life. It is said: I am present in my room; ten or twenty people are present in that building. But the room, or the building have nothing to do with the case. They remain what they are, even if no one is there. And if human beings have no

[16] En. 2 Ps. 30, s.3,4. Cf. En. Ps. 52,8.

[17] En. Ps. 144,22.

relationships at all to one another, which is often the case in a block of flats, then it becomes difficult to speak of presence. It is even worse if people pass by each other indifferently, or even if they hate one another. It might be possible to call living in the same house "material presence", but true presence is something else. True presence presupposes a conscious and voluntary relationship between at least two people, as we find it in love. That is: being in the presence of another person through one's own personality. In the process, the boundary lines between the people do not disappear. Neither of the persons who is in the presence of the other loses his or her personality, but there is openness for one another. True presence includes reciprocity.

In the beginning of his *Confessions,* Augustine asks the question: how can I invoke or call God into me if he encompasses all things and is present in all creation? If God is already present in every human being – and, thus, in me, as well – how can I call God into me? The question thus becomes "To where do I call you, because I am in you, after all?"[18] Here Augustine does not answer the question directly. He does that in a later work. He then writes: it is true that God, as Creator and maintainer of all that exists, is present in everything and everyone. He cites the text of Paul: "God is not far from any of us. For in him, we live, we move, and we are" (Acts 17:27-28). According to Augustine, it should be possible to understand this text as applying to the material world, because even our bodies move and are in God. What is not in God? But Paul also says: "For everything is from him, through him, and in him" (Romans 11,36). But, on the basis of the words "God is not far" and "I am always with you," (Psalm 73:23), Augustine believes that Paul has a deeper, more spiritual meaning in mind: not so much being "in" God, but being "with" God. The ideal is to be with God, because only then is there reciprocal presence.

"Not all people are with God in the way meant when the psalmist says to God: I am always with you (Ps. 73:23), nor is he

[18] Conf. 1,2,2.

with all in the way meant when we say: The Lord be with you (Ruth 2:4). It is the great misfortune of human beings not to be with God, without whom we cannot be. Obviously he is not without God in whom he is. And yet if the human being fails to remember and understand and love God, he is not with God".[19]

Here it is a matter of not being "with" God, due to humankind's forgetfulness of God. For human beings can violate the relationship with God: "If we lose him, this is not to be attributed to the absence of him, who is everywhere, but because we turn away from him". For this reason, the psalmist prays – when his soul turns toward God due to a change in his life – that God will turn toward him.[20] God distances himself only from someone who distances him- or herself from him. God remains present, but the human being is not in his presence. Such a one-sided presence is certainly not God's intent with creation. But to those who love him, God grants the joy of his presence. God wants a response, a response of our love to his love. For this reason, we find, in the text of Augustine, such expressions as "being mindful, taking notice, loving" as the preconditions for a reciprocal presence. As a result of love, we must remain steadfast in the presence of our greatest good, God, and adhere to him, through whom we exist, in order to enjoy his presence. If he were absent, then we could not exist.[21]

Precisely by these means do human beings become the temple in which God dwells.[22] The temple of God is, once again, an image to express God's presence. A temple or church building has, no doubt, this symbolic significance. But it is characteristic of Augustine that he wants to go deeper. God's presence in a building, namely a church, remains, in the final analysis, one-sided. God seeks of humanity a freely given loving response. A building does not respond. So, ultimately, it is the human person who is at

[19] Trin. 14,12,16.
[20] En. Ps. 6,5.
[21] Trin. 8,4,6.
[22] S. Dom. m. 2,5,17.

issue: we, ourselves, must become God's temple, or his house, according to Paul's words: "We are God's temple" (1 Corinthians 3:17. 2 Corinthians 6:16). In a sermon on the occasion of the dedication of a church building, Augustine impresses upon the hearts of the faithful that this building is, indeed, the house for our prayers, but that the most important aspect is: being, ourselves, God's house. Just as the construction of a church requires a good deal of time, the building of oneself as a temple of God lasts throughout an entire lifetime; our consecration will only take place after this life.[23] The expression "the holy place of God" may refer to the area for prayer, and that is the way most people understand it. But Augustine chooses the interpretation that we cannot seek God's holy place without being involved in the quest ourselves. God makes a temple for himself in human beings who are of one heart.[24] God resides in his saints. God's temple is not a house with a lot of marble, a fine atrium, and shimmering ceilings; rather, he resides in the humble, peaceable human being who quakes in awe before the words of God (Isaiah 66:2).[25] Worshipping God in a temple means worshipping him in ourselves, because through him, we are made his temple. If we want to pray to God, then we must pray in ourselves, but we must take care that we are, indeed, a temple for God. It is through love of God and our neighbor that we are God's seat.[26] In point of fact, God requires no temple, but the temple requires God. But, God's temple, which is the human being, is not something static. When Augustine interprets the text "I shall worship you (bowing low) toward your holy temple" (Psalm 5:8), he interprets the word "toward" in the sense of "spiritual nearness", we must become, to an ever greater degree, the temple of God, and become, from an imperfect, to a perfect temple of God.[27]

[23] S. 336,1,1.
[24] En. Ps. 67,7.
[25] En. Ps. 92,6.
[26] Io. Eu. tr. 15,25. En. Ps. 98,4. En. Ps. 137,4.
[27] S. Dolbeau, Analecta Bolland. 110 (1992), p. 299. En. Ps. 5,9.

Thus, God's presence in a temple or a church differs appreciably from his presence in the faithful. This latter differs from his general presence in the world or in non-believers. In the faithful, God's presence acquires the special name "indwelling". God does not dwell within those who do not honor or thank him (cf. Romans 1:21). God is, indeed, present everywhere, but he does not dwell in all, because the person who does not possess the Spirit of God, does not belong to God (Romans 8:9). Augustine draws a distinction here between the presence of the Godhead and the grace of the indwelling. The grace of dwelling within comes only to the one whom he made his temple. But, then, he does not dwell in all the faithful in precisely the same way. That depends upon the degree of holiness. The light is, indeed, the same, but those who approach the light most closely and want to see it obtain the most light. The same applies to listening; one believer listens better to God's word than the other.[28]

The foregoing thoughts clearly show that praying, as an act of faith, is played out within the context of reciprocal presence.

4. Giving Back God's Word

Thus far, we have stressed, repeatedly, the passive aspect of praying. But, we must be cautious with the use of the word "passive." Passive may mean that one simply undergoes something, or that something overcomes us, against our will. That is the case if we say: I am getting sick, I am beaten, I am struck by adversity. These are all things we would rather not experience. We find an altogether different form of passivity in expressions such as: I was overcome by the beauty of a painting, or by someone's goodness. In that case, too, something happens to me that I did not make myself, but it is not against my will. On the contrary, I am happy about it, and I stand open to it. I experience it as a

[28] Ep. 187,5,16-6,19 and 8,29.

gift. But a gift requires the presence of a recipient, because nothing can be given if there is no one to receive it. Receptiveness is our active contribution in everything that is given to us. We must not underestimate receptiveness, for it constitutes at least half of our existence, and it is not as easily practiced as one might think.

Augustine applies these thoughts to prayer. We have already seen how our praying is based upon the Holy Scriptures and how we can read the Bible entirely as God's speaking to us. There, God informs us of himself and teaches us how to pray to him. Christ, too, taught us how to pray to him with the Our Father. In that sense, praying is giving God's words back to him. For that reason, we must be careful with the expression "I pray". It sounds so normal, but it hides the danger of individualism within itself. If I regard prayer merely as my personal activity, then I lose sight of the receptive character of prayer. In addition, there is the danger that I neglect the communal dimension of praying. It seems to me not to be an exaggeration to say that, strictly speaking, there is no individual prayer, which is not to say that no personal prayer exists. This apparent contradiction becomes solved if we consider that faith is not our own project, but we have received it from others. Our present belief stands upon a long tradition of Jews and Christians who lived before us.

"Let us all address our soul, because on account of our common faith all of us have but one soul. All of us who believe in Christ form one single person in virtue of the unity of his body".[29]

Even the content of our prayer is based upon tradition. We pray with words, inner feelings, lamentations and longings of countless predecessors in the faith. All the longing of many generations before us is present in our praying. We pray with the words of the Bible. We pray together with the entire Body of Christ because Christ himself prays in and through his body:

[29] En. 1 Ps. 103,2.

> "On whatever day I call upon you, hear me quickly... Peter prayed, Paul prayed, the other apostles prayed, the faithful prayed in these early days, the faithful prayed in the ages that followed, the faithful prayed in the time of the martyrs, the faithful pray in our own time, and the faithful will pray in the days of our descendants".[30]

What, then, becomes of personal prayer or personal receptiveness? Must we merely, in an impersonal way, repeat what others have prayed? Clearly not, and for that reason, I have drawn the distinction between individualistic and personal prayer. Augustine says that we must learn how to pray with our own voice. By that he means we must make the words of the Bible our "own" so that they become "our" words: "Many call to God, not with their own voice, but with the voice of their bodies; not with the emotion of their hearts, but with the sound from their lips."[31] Parrots can also bring forth sounds, but that is not enough; we must pray consciously, with a pure heart.[32] This appropriation is also necessary because the language of prayer, in the various periods of our history, is subject to change. Indeed, that applies to the circumstances and needs of the time in which we live as well. But even if we arrive at a distinct and personal prayer, God remains the source of its inspiration.

For Augustine, both belief and prayer are gifts of God. "You cannot pray with faith if you have no faith...Thus, from God's gifts you give to God. God receives from you that which he gave you". Even the fact that we stand as beggars in God's presence is a gift of his. That is why the text goes on to say: "If he had not first given, your state of beggar would remain totally senseless".[33] In prayer, thus, we return God's gifts to him. God listens in us for his own voice. When Augustine interprets a psalm for us in which we are invited to rejoice before God, he asks his listeners to join him in considering the words of the psalm attentively. The words

[30] En. Ps. 101,3.
[31] En. Ps. 141,2.
[32] En. 2 Ps. 18,1.
[33] S. 168,5,5.

must bring forth seeds in our hearts, which must, in turn, yield fruit. In this way, God wants to hear his own voice echoed:

> "Whatever instrument God's voice employs, God's voice it is always. Nothing but his own voice sounds sweetly in his ears. When we speak we delight him, as long as he speaks through us".[34]

The confession that Augustine wants to make before God's countenance (that is: in God's presence) is one he will make silenctly yet not silently; silently insofar as sound is concerned, yet crying out love's longing. If Augustine says anything good to people, then he said it first to God. And then there follows a short sentence that is important for praying:

> "Or do you hear, God, sometimes, something good told by me that you did not tell me before?"[35]

God's speech thus precedes the speech of human beings with God. The prior speech of God has the clear goal that God wants to draw human beings toward himself and bring human beings into relationship with himself. Another goal is: to lead human beings to self-knowledge. "For hearing something from you about oneself, what is that other than becoming acquainted with oneself?"[36]

5. Introspection and Interiority

The expression "the inner person" is Augustine's most general description of the whole inner nature of the human being. In order to indicate the internal human being, he also frequently uses the terms: the spirit, the soul, or the heart of the human being. As we have already seen, he calls our hearts: the house of God, God's temple, or God's field. To these we could add: the bridal chamber or the bed-chamber of God, God's seat, the treasure chest in

[34] En. Ps. 99,1.
[35] Conf. 10,2,2.
[36] Conf. 10,3,3.

which God's riches dwell.[37] Blessing the Lord with all your inner being is the same as praising the Lord with all your spirit, soul, or heart. The internal stands opposite the external. The external is not without significance, but outer impressions and experiences must be received and processed by the internal. The external must serve, or be the expression of the internal. No fewer than seven times do we find in Augustine's Rule a transition from the external to the internal; from praying with the mouth to praying with the heart, from physical hunger to the spiritual hungering for the Word of God, from not wanting to please through clothing, to pleasing through a good life, from seeing externally, to inner longing, from a physical wound to a wound of the heart, from outward appearance to having a good character, from granting forgiveness with words to forgiving from the heart.

Internal life requires introspection. Because God is present in all his creatures – and in quite a particular way in the case of human beings who are created in his own image – Augustine regularly calls upon us to turn inwardly, toward our hearts. To this end, he points toward Isaiah 46:8 "Turn back to your hearts".

"Return to the heart. Why do you go away from yourselves? Why do you travel lonely ways? You go astray by wandering about. Return. Where? To the Lord. But it is too early. First, return to your heart. Outside, you are wandering, having become a stranger to yourself. You do not know yourself, and you seek him by whom you are made. Return, return to the heart. … Return to your heart. See there perhaps what you perceive about God because the image of God is there. In the inner self Christ dwells. In your inner self you are renewed according to the image of God. In his image recognize its author".[38]

What is striking in this text is the fact that we do not reach God directly, but that we must proceed first by way of our hearts. That requires a great deal of effort. The temptation to pursue things outside oneself is great. Due to the fact that we are not

[37] Conf. 8,8,19. En. Ps. 35,5. En. Ps. 45,9. En. Ps. 92,6. En. Ps. 63,11.
[38] Io. Eu. tr. 18,10.

purely spiritual beings, we need the material world around us in order to be able to exist. But that is where the danger lies, namely that the human being could pass him- or herself by. Augustine describes this aptly, as follows:

> "People go to admire lofty mountains, and huge breakers at sea, and crashing waterfalls, and vast stretches of ocean, and the dance of the stars. But they leave themselves behind out of sight, and do not admire their inner selves".[39]

The human being turns back to his or her heart, and from there, he or she turns back toward God. Christ went away from our eyes so that we might return to our hearts and find him.[40] Turning inward toward one's own heart does not necessarily mean discovering the true God there, for it is possible that one ends up at an entirely human image of God, or with a god cut to human measurement. The true God remains at all times incomprehensible and unspeakable. He surpasses every human concept. Augustine himself, at one time, sought God not according to the insight of the spirit, but according to the senses of the flesh, to discover then: "You, however, were more internal than the most profound depths of my inner being, and higher than my greatest height".[41] And, because God is even more internal than our own hearts, there is no place to which we can flee without his being there. Wherever we go, we take ourselves along. We cannot flee from ourselves, and thus, we cannot flee from God, who is present in our deepest being.[42]

With respect to the topic of entering within our own hearts, we, ourselves are at issue, as well as God. The appeal to that end means the same to Augustine as "Do not surrender your soul. Rather, turn back and know yourself." To be good yourself, you must call in the "Allgood" within.[43] "Not desiring to be absent

[39] Conf. 10,8,15.
[40] En. Ps. 55,10. Conf. 4,12,19.
[41] Conf. 3,6,11.
[42] En. Ps. 74,9.
[43] En. 1 Ps. 70,14. S. 13,3.

from God; not desiring to be absent from oneself".[44] Someone who is in touch with his or her inner self seeks answers from him- or herself in the first place. Someone of that kind asks him- or herself: where am I headed and how do I proceed? Is my love well-directed? What am I seeking and what is my response to it? One asks these questions of oneself not to stop short at oneself, but to ascend outside oneself. That is why Augustine frequently links interiority with self-knowledge. A person does not usually wish to see his or her own faults. Augustine attempts: "How much has a person within himself that he never digs up, how often does a person seek within himself, only to come up empty-handed?" People churn the ground up in the hope of finding gold, but many do not heed the words "I shall search my spirit" (Psalm 77:7). They do not question or assess themselves, because they are afraid to do so.[45] But God, who dwells within us shows us who we are; by his word he gives us self-knowledge. Here, Augustine employs the image that we all put ourselves behind our backs, because we do not want to look at ourselves. But God fetches us out from there and places us before our own eyes, so that we must see ourselves.[46] God poses no threat, because he always speaks the truth:

> "I beg you, my Lord, not to answer me with silence. Speak to me yourself in my heart in truth, for you alone speak so. Then let me retire in my private room and sing my songs of love to you".[47]

But God does more than give us self-knowledge. In a tender way, he also works on our hearts, and creates order there. "Lord, with a very tender and merciful hand, you have shaped and ordered my heart."[48] Order means rest. In prayer we find rest with God. "Turn back to your hearts, you who have fallen by the wayside, and cling to him who made you. Stay with him and you will find

[44] En. Ps. 39,27.
[45] En. Ps. 76,9.
[46] Conf. 8,7,16. En. Ps. 74,9.
[47] Conf. 12,16,23.
[48] Conf. 6,5,7.

solid ground. Rest in him, and you will rest easy".[49] Prayer provides not only rest, it also alleviates our loneliness, for in our hearts we find God and Christ.

"Let Christ speak to you within where no human being is. Even if someone is at your side, no one is in your heart. This does not mean that absolutely nobody should be in your heart. Let Christ be in your heart. Let his anointing be in your heart, so that your heart may not be thirsting in a desert with no springs by which it may be watered".[50]

The emphasis placed upon turning inward, upon the heart, and upon interiority also has a direct consequence for our prayer. In prayer, it is a matter of God as well as oneself. Ultimately, God does not ask for our gifts, such as gold, incense, or myrrh, expensive things from the East, or a calf and a lamb from the fold. God asks for ourselves. The sacrifice we are called upon to make is one we carry within ourselves:

> "My prayer to the God of my life is within me (Ps. 42,9). Here within me I have the victim I must offer, here within me the incense I must burn, here within me is the sacrifice with which I may move my God".[51]

When our hearts are lifted up to God, then our hearts are God's altar, at which we dedicate his gifts to us and ourselves to him, and give them back. On it we also bring the sacrifice of our humility and praise.[52] The strong emphasis on interiority could perhaps give the impression that Augustine was always occupied with himself. But turning inwardly, within the heart, is not, in his case, narcissism, nor a mirroring of the self, where all that matters is one's own ego. Augustine's intention goes much deeper. When he says: "Do not keep your heart within your own heart"[53], he is protesting, with these words, against a false interpretation of interiority.

[49] Conf. 4,12,18. S. 47,14,23.
[50] Ep. Io. tr. 3,13.
[51] En. Ps. 41,17.
[52] Ciu. 10,3,2.
[53] En. Ps. 61,14.

The goal of turning within oneself is precisely to be able to turn outwards, to ascend above one's own ego, to leave one's ego, to open oneself to God and one's neighbor.

6. Concentration (intentio) and Attention (attentio)

In order to experience prayer as interiority and presence, stillness is required. For Augustine, stillness has two meanings. It can have the literal meaning of absence of sound and noise, as in the following text: "If you come to a quiet, restful, and pleasant place, then say: let us pray here. You find the order that prevails at that spot pleasant, and you believe that God can hear you there clearly".[54] In a discussion of the psalm verse "I was mindful for endless years" (Psalm 77:6) Augustine asks himself whether this is not the same as "the great silence". Whoever wants to think of endless years must find inner rest within his or her heart, far from all the tumult that comes from the outside, and far from all the turmoil that human affairs entail.[55] In this text, the other meaning of stillness comes to the fore, namely the spiritual stillness within the human heart. For there is in us a certain conflict between attachment to this life and our inner religious conviction, as Paul writes in Romans 7:22-23: "In my inner being, I take pleasure in God's law, but in my limbs, I am aware of another law that wages war against the law of my reason and delivers me captive to the supremacy of sin over my limbs". On this point, Augustine says:

> "In our silence something sounds softly to us from above, reaching not our ears but our minds. Any who hear that song are so disenchanted with material noise that the whole of human life seems to them a confused uproar, which stops them hearing a sound from above that is delightful, a sound like no other and beyond description".[56]

[54] En. 2 Ps. 33,8.
[55] En. Ps. 76,8.
[56] En. Ps. 42,7.

Since our hearts are restless because of the many things they long for, they require, in order to seek God, a certain simplicity, and quiet, free time; not the rest of idleness, but the rest of our capacity to think.[57] This brings Augustine to the topic of concentration and attention. Concentration means: directing our attention somewhere, directing the intellect in a focused way toward something, collecting oneself around one central point. Concentration is thus the movement of the heart or of the spirit, which gathers and unifies itself, which is particularly necessary if the human being directs him- or herself to the one God. Therefore, the orientation of our hearts must be simple, based upon a simple love. Concentration in praying renders our hearts serene and pure.[58] Gathering together and forming one unified whole stand in opposition to the fragmentation to which we are, of necessity, exposed because we live in a multiplicity of temporal matters and worries. And yet, this gathering together constitutes a portion of our lives in this world because it entails that we are still en route toward a goal we have not yet reached. Augustine describes how he experiences his life as fragmentation and distraction. But between the one God and us, many people involved in many things and held captive by many things, stands Jesus Christ. Because we are grasped by him, we can grasp the palm through him. Not scattered, but gathered together and purposeful we reach toward the palm of our heavenly calling (cf. Phil. 3:12-14), where we shall hear the sound of God's praise.[59]

The concentration opens out into attention. Attention means being in the presence of one thing or person with our thoughts and consciousness. After the process of gathering, we arrive at God, with whom we wish to come into contact. We want to think of him, and, as much as possible, only of him. Before we arrive at the one God, we do, indeed, require many things in this life. Do they then suddenly disappear? No, the strange thing is that precisely this turning toward and attention for the one God

[57] Vera rel. 35,65.

[58] S. Dom. m. 2,3,11-14.

[59] Conf. 11,29,39. En. Ps. 38,6.

causes us to reach farther and broadens us. To put it in Augustine's words: "cause our hearts to expand or enlarge". We can compare this with the beautiful text by a Flemish mystic, whose name is not known:

> "All things /Are too narrow for me
> I am so broad!/I have grasped
> For an uncreated thing/In eternal time."[60]

The one God causes us to reach farther without causing the many things to distract us, or cut us off from him, who encompasses everything. This process now already begins. It finds its perfection when the one God will be everything for us.[61] We find this thought everywhere, wherever Augustine talks of the love that expands our hearts. Precisely by orienting ourselves in love toward the one God, we acquire more interest, attention, and care for more things and human beings than if we orient ourselves toward limited earthly goods. In the One, we meet the many, because love of God includes the love of one's neighbors: "Where the practice of compassion is concerned, it would appear obvious that someone who loves his neighbor can regard no one as a stranger".[62]

In praying, we thus free our spiritual view or the attention of our hearts of many transitory things and concerns. In that sense, Augustine understands the admonition from the Sermon on the Mount: "When you pray, go to your inner chamber, close the door behind you, and pray to your Father, who is in Heaven" (Matthew 6:6). Our hearts are the inner chamber (bedroom or bridal chamber). Closing the door after ourselves means leaving all earthly concerns behind us, because a lot of images of the imagination that have nothing to do with the matter in hand, images of temporal and visible things, try to drown out the voice of the one at prayer. If we know how to keep them out, our concentration becomes one and single-minded. That means: turning away from all the tumult

[60] Text in S. AXTERS, Mystiek Brevier III, p. 234. Antwerpen, 1946.
[61] S. 255,6,6.
[62] En. 18,2 Ps. 118. En. 10,6 Ps. 118. En. 14,2-4 Ps. 118.

and the obstacles that come from without, in order to call to God in the inner chamber, where no one sees us.[63] Closing the door also refers to our attitude toward worldly goods. This door has two parts: one is the longing for earthly goods, the other is the fear of earthly calamity[64]. Closing the door is closing the heart before evil, because sometimes the heart acts against itself by desiring evil. We close our door whenever we go inside, into the greatest depths of our consciousness, and we do not expect the goods of this world from God, but rather, inner goods. Someone who wishes to please human beings and seeks his or her own praise, does not close the door.[65] But this does not mean, by any means, that we can set the limits of our hearts around ourselves. We must never encapsulate our hearts or seal them within a wall. We must not shut up our hearts within our hearts, but rather, we must lift them up to God. We do this by appealing to him, confessing our sins to him, by thanking him, by placing our hope in him. In the process, Augustine refers to the psalm verse "Pour out your hearts before God" (Psalm 62:9). If we pour out our hearts before God, we do not lose our hearts. God catches them up. For that reason, we can be hopeful of casting all our cares at him.[66]

With respect to the consideration that we never quite manage to shut out our daily worries from our prayers, we shall return to that later. Perhaps it is good, at this juncture, to say that we take our worries with us to God, and allow them to disappear in him, that is, that we entrust them to him. In this way, God can become, for a few moments, the central point of our concentration. That is the turning of our hearts (*conversio cordis*) toward God, on which all praying is based. Prayerful attention thus comes into being as a result of a double movement, one of turning away and letting go, and one of turning toward or surrender. Both movements find their origin in love.

[63] En. 2 Ps. 34,3.
[64] En. Ps. 141,3-4.
[65] En. Ps. 35,1 and 5.
[66] En. Ps. 61,14.

7. The Short Prayer

At one place in his works, Augustine mentions the short prayer. He had heard that the monks in the Egyptian desert said many short prayers. The words were spoken as if they were arrows, shot off quickly, and hence the name, short or ejaculatory prayers. They were intended not to allow the keenly honed concentration, which is essential to prayer, to flag and grow dull through longer interruptions. In this way, the Egyptian monks show conclusively that concentration should not be disrupted too quickly if it persists. On the other hand, concentration must not be put on to the point of boredom, if it cannot be maintained.[67] Thus, the short prayer is a component part of continuous praying.

[67] Ep. 130,10,20.

III. Prayer as Longing

1. Prayer as an Exercise in Longing

Human beings are creatures of longing. All kinds of longings keep us in motion and drive us onward. Living is longing. It is typical that our earth-bound longings for riches, honor, sensual pleasure, or health, cannot ultimately satisfy us, because they are of a temporal and transitory nature. Human longing grasps higher.[1]

When Augustine speaks of praying, he shows a clear preference for the word "longing." Longing is the heart of prayer, so that Augustine can say: "Your longing is your prayer".[2] Whoever has no longing remains dumb before God.[3] Longing is an aspect of both hoping and loving. People who love one another long for each other. And yet, longing has a character all its own. Longing is an inner movement of the heart that reaches out to absent things or persons. "Longing is nothing more than desiring things that are absent."[4] Wherever we experience and regret the absence of something good, a longing arises to possess the good, or, perhaps more aptly, to have it in one's presence. It is in that sense that Augustine interprets the words of the Song of Songs 5:8, "I am wounded by love," for as long as we long for something and do not yet possess it, one can call that longing the wound of love.[5] In this respect, longing differs from a love that derives joy from present things or persons, because then the longing is fulfilled. Longing is thus an "extension" of our hearts: it makes our hearts wider and makes it reach out for the goods that are longed for, goods that still lie, for

[1] En. Ps. 126,12.
[2] En. Ps. 37,14.
[3] En. Ps. 86,1.
[4] En. 8,4 Ps. 118.
[5] S. 298,2,2.

the time being, far removed.[6] And there are many spiritual goods that we must wait for, for which our longing must remain alive:

> "Eternal benefits, on the other hand, are first and foremost eternal life itself, the imperishability and immortality of flesh and soul, the company of angels, the heavenly city, a permanent dignity, a Father and a homeland, the one beyond death and the other beyond enemies. We should be longing for these benefits with infinite desire, pray for them with tireless perseverance, not with long speeches but with the ardour of our desire. Desire is praying always, even if the tongue is silent. If you desire always, you are praying always. When does prayer nod off to sleep? When desire grows cold. So let us beg for these everlasting benefits with insatiable eagerness; let us seek these good things with deep concentration. They benefit those who have them, and they cannot do them harm".[7]

The danger that precisely in the spiritual area, our longing could cool, is a great one. This longing rises above our daily activities of waking and sleeping, eating and drinking, developing strengths and becoming weary, being young, and growing old. Faith, hope, and love are not visible things.[8] That is why Augustine speaks of the "flame of longing","burning with longing", "the impatience of longing", "fervent longings".[9] Longing for God is not something that is given to us once and for all time. It has a beginning and it must grow continually. In a sermon, Augustine says: "That I might bring the longing in your hearts into motion, beloved. That it might grow in you". Our longing must constantly grow because we are not Christians if we do not desire God as our future.[10] Augustine regards love as the heart of Christian life. Without longing, there is no love. We frequently find the combination: "Let us long and love". The expression "The longing prays" alternates with "Love prays".[11] Other phrases go in the same direction:

[6] En. Ps. 39,3.
[7] S. 80,7.
[8] En. Ps. 38,10.
[9] En. Ps. 127,10. En. Ps. 126,1. En. Ps. 41,6. En. 20,3 Ps. 118.
[10] Io. Eu. tr. 18,7 Io. Ev. tr. 40,10. En. Ps. 91,1.
[11] Ep. Io. tr. 6,8.

"Longing is the womb of the heart" and "Longing is the thirst of the soul".[12] Thus, Augustine can describe the whole life of a Christian as one "holy longing".

"Let us return to that anointing of his, let us return to that anointing that teaches within what we cannot speak. Because you cannot see now, let your task be found in longing. The whole life of a good Christian is a holy longing. But what you long for you do not yet see; nevertheless, by longing you are made capacious so that when the time to see what you desire has come, you may be completely filled... So God by delaying, stretches the longing, by longing stretches the soul, by stretching makes it capacious. Let us long, sisters and brothers, because we are going to be filled...This is our life, that we should be trained by longing. But holy longing trains us to the extent that we have pruned our longings away from the love of this world".[13]

This holy longing can be present at all times. On the admonition "Pray without holding back" (1 Thessalonians 5:17), Augustine comments that our bodies are not capable of praying with words without interruption, or of remaining in a suppliant posture for long periods of time. Only an uninterrupted longing can always pray.

"The psalmist says: All my desire is before you, Lord. Not before human beings, who cannot see my heart, but before you is all my desire. Let your desire too be before him, and there your Father, who sees in secret, will reward you. This very desire is your prayer, and if your desire is continuous your prayer is continuous too. The apostle meant what he said: Pray without ceasing (1 Thess. 5:17). But can we be on our knees all the time, or can we prostrate our bodies continuously, or be holding up our hands uninterruptedly? No. If we say that these things constitute prayer, I do not think we can pray without ceasing. But there is an other kind of prayer that never ceases, an interior prayer, that is desire. Whatever else you may be engaged upon if you are all the while

[12] Io. eu. tr. 40,10. En. Ps. 62,5. En. Ps. 41,2.

[13] Ep. Io. tr. 4,6.

desiring that eternal Sabbath, you never cease to pray. If you do not want to interrupt your prayer, let your desire be uninterrupted. Your continuous desire is your continuous voice. You will only fall silent if you stop loving... The chilling of love is the silence of the heart. The blazing of love is the heart's clamor. If your love abides all the time, you are crying out all the time. If you are crying out all the time, you are desiring all the time. If you are desiring, you are remembering rest".[14]

In these texts, prayer appears as an exercise in longing for God, longing to be united with him in a manner that cannot be expressed. We must, over a long period of time, long for him, whom we shall possess in eternity, without becoming tired or giving up. The defferring of the gift serves to make us more receptive. Goods that are acquired easily often lose their value, because something good that has been awaited for a long time gives more joy.[15] That is why there is a certain degree of unrest in all longing. The history of salvation shows us that longing for God and Christ never rests. The lives of all the faithful, from the beginning of our history to its end, was and will be characterized by longing. The prophets and kings of the first Covenant longed, Simeon longed, and even the community of the faithful today, the Church, lives to the end of time, lives with the unrest of holy longing.[16]

And yet, longing is not an activity for which we must thank ourselves alone, and thus, we cannot simply attribute it to ourselves. Augustine frequently uses the expression "dragged along by longing."[17] This passive form means that all forms of longing have something reminiscent of being carried along about them, because they are based upon something attractive. The attractive aspects are the valuable and good things that arouse our longing. Human beings can, of course, be mistaken in what is valuable and good. They are mistaken when they regard harmful things, such as drink

[14] En. Ps. 37, 14.
[15] En. Ps. 83,3. S. 61,5,6.
[16] En. 20,1 Ps. 118.
[17] En. Ps. 38,6. En. Ps. 83,8.

and drugs, unbridled sex and unchecked self-seeking, as good. But it is always through a certain attractiveness outside ourselves that our longing is put into motion. It is put into motion in order to receive and to be fulfilled.

There is another "passive" aspect. Longing increases all the time because as a result of longing, our longing becomes greater, stronger, and more intense. If we have recognized something as desirable and worth striving for, we long for it more and more. The better we become acquainted with a certain good, the more we feel ourselves attracted to it. But we, ourselves, do not create the power of attraction ourselves; it is given to us. Thus, we are recipients rather than creators. In a well-known passage, Augustine describes how we are attracted by the truth, good fortune, righteousness, love, life, by Christ and God, and only those who love and experience longing can understand that. Then he illustrates this point by a few examples from daily life: show a sheep a green twig and you will attract it; show nuts to a child, and it feels attracted. He then concludes: "If you do not feel attracted (by God's great gifts), then pray that you will be attracted. Give me someone who loves, and he or she will sense what I am talking about… Give me someone who longs for something, and he or she will know what I am saying".[18] The emphasis on longing and love in this text has particular significance. Love has the power of identification, so that a person becomes, to a certain extent, that which he or she loves. "As one loves, so is one, too. If you love the earth, then you are the earth. If you love God – shall I dare say it? – you are God. I dare not say it of my own accord, but the Scriptures say it: 'I say: you are gods, sons of the All-Highest, all of you' (Psalm 82:6)".[19] Whoever loves goodness becomes good; whoever loves evil becomes bad. The same applies to longing. Through singing and praying, a human being becomes what he longs for. "If someone has sung the praises of earthly goods, transcending them, let him rejoice, for he is what

[18] Io. Eu. tr. 26,2-5.
[19] Ep. Io. tr. 2,14.

he has sung. Someone who sang while he is bound on the earth, let him wish to be what he has sung".[20] The opposition lies here between rejoicing and wishing.

God himself put the imprint of longing for him upon us.[21] He has cast his gaze upon our longing. For that reason, we must first listen for his voice, which warns and comforts us from on high, because it is the voice of him who for us takes the place of our earthly father and mother when they have left us.[22] The longing of love is a preparation for our sojourn with God (cf. John 14:3). Christ makes us ready for himself, and he keeps himself ready for us. He prepares a place for himself in us and a place for us within himself.[23] The final goal of our longing is God himself, who first gave us the promise that he would give himself. Because he first gave himself, he will also give himself as our future. As an immortal he will give himself to us when we have become immortal, because in the mortal Jesus did he give himself to mortal human beings.[24] Thus, the ultimate goal of our longing becomes continually more and more visible, namely union with God.

2. Praying in Faith, Hope, and Love

It is characteristic of Augustine that he knows how to preserve the unity between praying and the entirety of Christian life so strongly. He will never separate prayer from the most important acts of Christian existence: believing, hoping, and loving. The external form in which our prayer is accomplished is of but moderate interest to him. In light of what is of most critical importance, everything else retreats into the background. All of Augustine's spirituality and theology revolves around faith, hope, and love,

[20] En. Ps. 38,1.
[21] S. 56,3,4.
[22] En. 2 Ps. 26,23.
[23] Io. Eu. tr. 67,3.
[24] En. Ps. 42,2.

which have, in the more recent tradition, acquired the title "godly or theological" virtues. The fact that they have acquired that title is not without reason. Firstly, because these virtues are gifts from God; secondly, because they bring us into contact with the person of God himself. The interpersonal character of "believing in God, hoping in him, and loving him" distinguishes them from all other virtues. Practicing moderation, being strong, just, understanding, humble, cheerful, honest, etc. is something we do, in the first instance, for our own benefit, developing our own being, and for the benefit of those we love most. They form our personality and turn us into good people, so that we are also capable of being good for others. Augustine then regards all these other virtues as forms of love. Healthy love of ourselves and our fellow human beings can, indeed, be linked with love of God. It could be said that they serve to express – or, according to Augustine, they are even the embodiment of our love of God. And yet, there remains a definite difference between the theological virtues and the other virtues. Believing in someone, placing hope in someone, and loving someone directly reflect our relationship to another person.

This has as its consequence that for Augustine, faith, hope, and love are much more than conditions or favorable circumstances for praying. In the case of other theologians, one sometimes reads that the theological virtues "inspire" our prayer. For Augustine, that is expressing it too weakly. Praying itself is an act of faith, of hoping, and loving. Faith, hope, and love "at work" are the heart of all praying. "God teaches us," says Augustine, "no other song than the song of faith, hope, and love, a strong belief in the invisible God, an unshakable hope, and a love which remains eternal, love that can do nothing but grow, whereas faith and hope will cease to exist".[25] Faith, hope, and love lead the person praying to God. The praying person is the person who believes, hopes, longs for, and considers what he or she must ask of the Lord in the Our Father.[26] Even if we have already found God as a result of faith,

[25] En. Ps. 91,1.

[26] Ep. 130,13,24.

hope keeps looking for him; and as far as love is concerned, it finds God through faith and longs to possess him as he is.[27] God demands no external goods of us, but he seeks ourselves. For this reason, we must offer him the goods of our hearts, namely faith, hope, and love. God himself gave us these goods and no one can take them from us.[28]

Faith, hope, and love belong together, inextricably united. Love is not without hope, hope is not without love, and neither is without faith. For this reason, praying is an activity of all three: "Faith believes, hope and love pray. But hope and love cannot exist without faith. Consequently, faith prays as well".[29] Longing continually with this faith, this hope, and this love, that is praying without ceasing.[30] Although the relationship between praying and the theological virtues was the topic of discussion in many previous texts, we nevertheless want to address each one of these virtues individually and briefly.

a) Faith

Faith plays a dual role in praying. In the first place, brings us into God's presence. As we have seen, God is, indeed, present with his creatures, and thus, he is present with all human beings, but not all human beings are with God. Due to the fact that God's presence is always hidden and veiled, it can come to awareness only in faith, for real presence is only where there is conscious contact between at least two people. In the second place, the relationship between faith and prayer becomes something altogether more evident if one considers that faith is more than the assumption of a number of truths. Faith encompasses many different acts, such as giving oneself away, commending oneself, knowing oneself to be protected and cared for, being conscious of being accepted by the other. Faith is thus much more than knowledge. It engages our

[27] En. Ps. 104,3.
[28] En. Ps. 55,19.
[29] Ench. 7,2-8,2.
[30] Ep. 130,9,18.

entire person and life. Believing means: giving oneself to a certain extent, in order to enter into the love of another. Let us just think of lovers who say to one another "I believe in you," because even human love requires faith and trust in one another. No one is master of another's love. Love is a gift. Also with respect to God, it is a matter of believing in his love: "And we, we have recognized the love that God has for us, and we believe in it" (1 John 4:16).

In the introduction to his *Confessions,* Augustine asks the question what comes first: invoking God or praisng God, knowing God in faith, or invoking God. Of these three acts, invoking – praising – believing, believing is, without further debate, the first, because:

> "Who invokes you without knowing you? Or should you be invoked first so that we may come to know you? But how can people invoke him in whom they do not believe? And how can they believe without a preacher (Rom. 10:14)? But Scripture tells us that those who seek the Lord will praise him, for as they seek they find him, and on finding him they will praise him. Let me seek you, Lord, even while I am invoking you, and invoke you as I believe in you. My faith invokes you, Lord, this faith which is your gift to me, which you have breathed into me through the humanity of your Son and the ministry of your preacher".[31]

The overriding importance of faith is evident in this text without further discussion. After faith, there follow the two distinct forms of praying: first, invoking, so it seems, because Augustine places invocation rather more on the side of seeking for God, while praising occurs after God has been found. Several texts affirm the priority of faith. Faith is the precursor of prayer; for this reason, candidates for baptism must first hear and learn the confession of the faith, and only after that, the Our Father. In any case, the confession of faith is part of the act of faith, while the Our Father belongs to praying.[32] Praying is longing, but no one longs for anything in which he or she does not believe. Whoever believes in

[31] Conf. 1,1,1.
[32] S. 56,1,1.

Christ longs for him.[33] Faith is the source of prayer, but the source does not cease to flow; the water from the source continues to flow in the brook. Thus, too, faith cannot be separated from prayer; it continues in the prayer.

"The reading of the holy gospel encourages us to pray and to believe...If faith falters, prayer perishes. I mean, who is going to pray for what he don't believe in?... And to show that faith is the fountainhead of prayer, and that the stream cannot run when the source of water dries up, Paul went on to say: How shall they invoke one in whom they do not believe (Rom. 10:14)? So in order to pray, let us believe. And in order that the very faith by which we pray may not fail, let us pray. Faith pours out prayer, prayer being poured out obtains firmness for faith".[34]

Against the Pelagians, who believe that they themselves, must first, of their own accord give faith to God and direct their prayers to him before God gives us his gifts, Augustine maintains that both faith and prayer are gifts of God. Only after faith is given us can we pray with faith because only faith prays.[35] There is nothing that we have not received (1 Corinthians 4: 7). Thus, we give to God precisely what is from him. God wants to receive his own gifts from us.

b) Hope

Hope arises wherever we wish to possess something good, yet our powers fall short of the mark to acquire it. Our daily lives offer many examples. We say, for example: I hope the weather will be good, I hope everything goes well, I hope that another will respond to my love. Our whole existence is borne along by hope. This reveals itself in the strongest way within our relationship with God. When Augustine describes praying as longing, he describes it as hope at the same time. Longing is not only an

[33] Io. Eu. tr. 67,3. Ep. Io. tr. 9,2.
[34] S. 115,1,1.
[35] S. 168,5,5-6,6.

aspect of love; it is also an aspect of hope. In his letter to Proba on prayer, Augustine writes: "Why dedicate yourself to prayer unless you place your hope in God?". In prayer, we thirst for God as long as we live in hope.[36] Because hope arises from the lack of a certain good, we can distinguish two aspects in it: one of sadness at the lack, and one of happiness due to the expectation of something good. This is stated beautifully in the *Confessions:*

> "If we could not weep into your very ears, no shred of hope would be left to us. How comes it that such sweet fruit is plucked from life's bitterness, the sweetness of groans, tears, sighs, and laments? Does the comfort lie in this, that we hope you will hear? This is certainly true of our prayers, for they presuppose a desire to reach you".[37]

Now, we are still living in the land of banishment, of temptations, sadness, and death. But, as long as we sojourn here, we must sing of God, who is our future, and long for him with patience. Patience exercises our longing[38]. As long as we wait patiently, we still sigh. But this sighing is never despair. It is mixed with the joy of hope. It is like the sighing of a woman giving birth; it is the sighing of a holy impatience. "We sigh with great hope. Sighing includes sadness, but there is also a sigh that contains joy. I think that the barren Sarah rejoiced when she sighed as she gave birth. We, too, were pregnant with fear of you, and yet, we gave birth to the spirit of salvation (cf. Isaiah 26:18)".[39] When we hope, we rejoice already.[40] Thus, in this life, hope is our greatest comfort because it anticipates the good that must yet come. Our songs of praise should be drenched with hope. It is from a position of hope that we sing the praises of God.[41]

"The children of human beings shall hope under the shelter of your wings (Ps. 57:2), for it is in hope that we have been saved

[36] Ep. 130,1,2 and 14,27.
[37] Conf. 4,5,10.
[38] Ep. Io. tr. 4,7.
[39] En. 1 Ps. 101,2.
[40] En. Ps. 145,9. En. 2 Ps. 31,20.
[41] En. Ps. 145,7.

(Rom. 8:24)...Here we are with hope suckling us, hope nourishing us; hope strenghtening us, and giving us consolation and comfort in this life of toil. It is in this hope that we sing alleluia. Just look what joy there is in hope. What will the reality itself be like?...We are thirsty, we are hungry, it must be that we shall be satisfied... Now the glory of our God, the glory of our Christ, is concealed, and with it is concealed ours also. But when Christ appears, your life, then you too will appear with him in glory (Col. 3:4). Then it will be alleluia in reality, while now it is just in hope. Hope sings it, love sings it".[42]

We hope for eternal life in God. For that reason alone are we, in fact, Christians, says Augustine.[43] But eternal happiness is no lonely adventure. We hope and pray that all others might reach joy with us. In the heavenly Jerusalem, we shall not be alone, but rather, it will be a numerous community.[44] Hope is thus no egoistic virtue that is nothing more than a form of concern about one's own happiness.

c) Love

Concerning love, Augustine says: "What is love but a life that unites, or attempts to unite, two things or two people, namely the person who loves, and the object of someone's love."[45] That is not only so in human relationships, but also in our relationship to God. In every love, we discover a double wave motion: one of striving for unity, and one of maintaining distance out of respect for the personality of the other. In point of fact, this is what Augustine means when he says: "Attempt to unite". Love never leads to full unity, in which one person would swallow up the other, because that would mean the destruction of one of the two. This applies with infinitely greater veracity in the case of our relationship with God, whose transcendence we must always respect.

[42] S. 255,5,5.
[43] Ciu. 6,9,5.
[44] En. Ps. 39,10.
[45] Trin. 8,10,14.

It is clear that here on earth, our love of God consists of longing, and not yet in satisfaction. Everything that we ask of the Father in this longing in the name of his only born Son he will grant us, at least, if this leads us to salvation.[46] Our quest for God is driven by a striving that we can translate as "longing." Augustine comments that this striving is not exactly the same as love, but nevertheless, striving and love belong to the same family.[47] He expresses the same thought in rich imagery: "Now it is a hungering love that sings alleluia, later it will be an enjoying love that sings it".[48]

Love belongs to the development of our humanity. There is no love that accomplishes nothing. But what it does may be evil, or good. Evil if it accomplishes all sorts of misdeeds, good if it accomplishes love of God and one's neighbor. There are so many strivings in the human heart. Thus, it is necessary to keep our love pure. That is a difficult process. In this regard, Augustine anticipates a despondent comment on the part of his listeners and responds to it: "Shall I then say: it would be better to love nothing? Far be that from me. If you love nothing, you will be dulled, dead, despicable, and miserable. Love, but be careful of what you love".[49] A person who does not love is cold and unfeeling.[50]

God has given us his love. When he asks that we should love him and our fellow human being for his sake, then, in point of fact, he is asking that what he has given be returned to him.[51] For this reason, we must pray for joy in the good, which is, in fact, the same thing as praying for the gift of love:

> "Anyone to whom God has granted sweetness, anyone in whom he graciously inspires a delight in what is good, must pray earnestly

[46] Io. eu. tr. 86,3.
[47] Trin. 9,12,18.
[48] S. 255,5.
[49] En. 2 Ps. 31,5.
[50] En. 2 Ps. 32, s.1,6.
[51] S. 297,1,1.

that this gift may be increased to such a point that its recipient not only learns to set little store by all other joys in comparison with this but is even prepared to endure any suffering for the sake of it. To speak more plainly, the person I have just described is one to whom God grants love: love for God, and love of neighbour on account of God".[52]

[52] En. 17,2 Ps. 118.

IV. Heart and Word

1. Oral Prayer, and Prayer of the Heart

"God, you called, you shouted, broke through my deafness. You flared, you blazed, banished my blindness. You lavished your fragance, I gasped, and now I pant for you, I tasted you, and I hunger and thirst, you touched me, and I burned for your peace".[1]

Here, Augustine talks about the spiritual senses of the heart: hearing, sight, taste, smell, and touching with the heart. Since Origen, this has been the accepted approach in the mystical literature. At issue here are images borrowed from our daily reality in order to describe something that is, in itself, indescribable. Precisely because our sight, hearing, taste, smell, and touch culminate in an immediate perception without the necessity of reasoning on an intellectual level, the images lend themselves quite well to expressing the many varied activities of our hearts. Augustine frequently talks about sight and hearing, trying and tasting with the heart. Thus, in a sermon, he says:

> "Above all pleasures, which include even lawful delights, we must love justice. You see, if you have got interior senses, all these interior senses are delighted by the delights of justice. If you have got interior eyes, observe the light of justice: For with you is the fountain of life, and in your light shall we see light (Ps. 36:10) and about that light the psalm says: Enlighten my eyes, lest I fall asleep in death (Ps. 13:4). If you have interior ears, try to hear justice. Such were the ears he was looking for, the one who said: Whoever has ears to hear, let him hear (Lk. 8:8). If you have an interior sense of smell, listen to the apostle: For we are the good odor of Christ for God everywhere (2 Cor. 2:15). If you have an interior sense of taste, listen to this: Taste and see that the Lord is sweet (Ps. 34:9).

[1] Conf. 10,27,38. See also 10,6,8.

> If you have an interior sense of touch, listen to what the bride sings about the bridegroom: His left hand is under my head, and his right hand embraces me (Sg. 2:6)... Let us see, my dear sisters and brothers – it can be any of you; I ask the question, and I wish that you answer what I am going to say – let us see whether you take such delight in justice that you prefer it to those other delights enjoyed by the bodily senses".[2]

The fact that these are images is clearly apparent when Augustine states: "The Lord is for our hearts, eyesight, and voice, smell and food. He stands for everything, because he is none of these things. And he is none of these things because he is the Creator of them all".[3] Certainly, Augustine does not intend to present any sort of materialistic view regarding God. And yet, he persists in using the images to show that even the spiritual has its own pleasures and joys. He intends to show that not only our senses experience enjoyment, but that there is also such a concept as spiritual pleasure. One need not convince anyone of the fact that life knows many physical pleasures, but it is necessary to convince people that the spiritual life has its own pleasures that bear some resemblance to sensory pleasures. In the process, Augustine refers to Psalm 35:8-10: "The children of human beings will hope under the protection of your wings; they will become inebriated from the surfeit from your house. You shall drench them with the stream of your pleasures, because the source of life is with you, and by your light we shall see the light". And to that, Augustine adds: "Give me someone who loves, and he or she will know what I say".[4] Pleasures do not disappear if we turn toward God, but they are changed. Praying, singing the psalms, reading the Scriptures, doing good deeds, the hope of the world to come, lifting up one's heart to God, appear to be difficult things, but they can all culminate in spiritual pleasures. Because, for the person who loves, bothersome

[2] S. 159,4,4.
[3] S. 28,2.
[4] Io. Eu. tr. 18,1. Io. Ev. tr. 26,4.

activities are not difficult. Love lightens burdens, and people is happy to do things they believe in.[5]

People who take no notice of God, or have not a correct view of God can, indeed, make noises to show that they are engaged in supplication, but they cannot lift up their voices to God. They cannot say: "my God," "my liberator". Believers can, indeed, do that, and that is a privilege. They have their hearts with God.[6]

In the second chapter of Augustine's Rule, we read the short sentence: "What you speak with your mouth you must also live in your hearts"[7]

"Your lips and your heart must be in agreement. If you seek peace from God, be reconciled with yourself. Let there be no harmful conflict between your mouth and your heart...Lord, you know that what my lips utter is also in my heart".[8]

It is a thought we frequently find in Augustine's works. Praying with one's heart has several meanings. An initial meaning is that our prayers must be forthright and sincere. If prayer remains an external act, it is no longer a reflection of our inner feelings, which prayer must be. A prayer that is merely said with the tongue, without the heart, is hollow and empty. Prayer is not a matter of speaking a great deal, but rather, of fiery devotion to God. We do not require many words, but we do need abiding affection.[9] Many people pray with their tongues, but remain dumb with their hearts. But there are also many people whose tongues are silent, but they call out with their affection.

God's ears are always attentive to human hearts.[10] If we pray with our hearts, it does not matter whether the prayer is offered with words or in silence:

[5] En. Ps. 74,1. Vid. 21,26.

[6] En. Ps. 139,10.

[7] See also chapter II.5 "Conversion and Interiority".

[8] En. Ps. 39,16.

[9] Ep. 130,10,19.

[10] En. Ps. 119,9.

> "When we pray to God, whether with our voice when that is appropriate, or in silence, we must cry to him from our heart. The cry of the heart is the mighty concentration of our thought, and when this takes place in prayer it expresses the mighty love of one who is longing and begging for the result he hopes will follow".[11]

We cannot always tell our fellow human beings what we want to, and sometimes it is better to be silent. But with God, we can even "speak in silence, with closed lips and a calling heart".[12] Our hearts are an "internal desert" where we are alone, in silence, with God. There we can examine our faith and see if our heart speaks when we say the prayer: "And forgive us our trespasses, as we forgive those who trespassed against us" (Matthew 6:12). For there in the desert there also run a few brooks with holy water, namely with what we know and remember from the holy Scriptures. There we are reminded of God's words, which we have heard or read.[13] In order to pray, we need not seek for a high, lonely mountain. Some people believe that they are closer to God on a high mountain. But then they forget that God is closest to the humble person. We must descend to the depths in order to reach the Almighty. A humble heart is that low place.[14]

The foregoing does not mean that Augustine underestimates praying with words, but it is, indeed, subordinate to the love and longing in one's heart. Words are necessary aids to put us into the correct frame of mind to pray, and to make us conscious of our longing. Words are indispensable, because we are human beings and not purely spiritual creatures. For this reason, it is necessary to pray with words at predetermined times to call our spirits back from our daily cares and activities. Even as a bishop, Augustine wanted to continue living in a monks' community because "he much preferred to do some manual labor every day at certain established times, as is the custom in well-run monasteries, and

[11] En. 29,1 Ps. 118.
[12] S. 357,4.
[13] S. 47, 14, 23.
[14] Io..Eu. tr. 15, 25.

have the remaining hours free for reading and prayer, or to discuss something from the holy Scriptures".[15]

To speak words is to give a sign to the outside of what one wants internally. We need not say any words to God to make our desires known to him, or to remind him of anything. We pray with our hearts, but God knows our hearts. Some people wonder: if God already knows everything, why must we nevertheless pray? The response to this question is complex, as will become apparent from what follows. Generally, we could say that we become aware of ourselves through prayer, aware of our own condition, and of our own needs in God's light. This applies to both the internal prayer and the prayers with words. Where it is a question of praying with words, we must consider that it also has a significance for others. In this way, others who hear us pray are awakened to lift themselves up to God. As a public occurrence, it must fulfill a social role, both within a monastic community[16] and the community of the faithful, as well as with respect to the outside world. But even for ourselves, praying with words is important. It was not for nothing that Jesus taught us the words of the Our Father. He taught them to us so that we might know how we must speak to God. Indeed, words guide us to the deeper reality that they signify.[17] This thought from an early dialogue of Augustine's with his son Adeodatus, we rediscover in Augustine's later works. We need not deal with God with words in order to obtain what we want, but rather, with our hearts, with the concentration of our thoughts, with a pure love and simple feelings. And yet, we must regularly be reminded with words of the reality that these words contain within themselves. Every prayer – whether internal or verbal – even if it does not serve the function of notifying God of anything – makes our hearts serene and pure, so that they become receptive to God's gifts. This receptiveness is lacking in some, because we easily allow ourselves to be caught up by temporal

[15] Op. Mon. 29, 37.
[16] En. Ps. 99, 12.
[17] Mag. 1, 20

matters. Prayer brings about a turning of our hearts to God, and renders the eye of the heart simple.[18]

"We also pray to God in words at certain fixed hours and times, so that we may urge ourselves on and take note with ourselves how much progress we have made in this desire, and may rouse ourselves more earnestly to increase it...Because that desire grows somewhat lukewarm by reason of our cares and preoccupations with other things, we call our mind back to the duty of praying at fixed hours, and we urge ourselves in the words of our prayer to press forward to what we desire. Otherwise, after our desire has begun to grow lukewarm, it then becomes entirely cold and is completely extinguished unless it is frequently rekindled".[19]

We, you and I, says Augustine, must be encouraged to pray. There is no other hope for us in the midst of all the evil in the world. We must not be destroyed through that evil. For that reason, God wanted us to ask in order to receive, to seek in order to find, to knock in order to be let inside (Matthew 7:7).[20]

Another meaning of praying with one's heart is to reach agreement between our praying and our deeds, between prayer and life. A good daily life renders our prayers truthful and valuable.

"Offer to God a sacrifice of praise (Ps. 50:14)...So on hearing this someone began to reflect in his own mind, and to say: I will get up each morning and go to church. I will sing one hymn in the morning and another in the evening, and a thirth or fourth at home. In this way I will offer a daily sacrifice of praise as a victim to God. Now you are doing certainly well, if you do that. But take care not to be over confident because you are doing it, for while your tongue is blessing God, your life may be cursing him". [21]

Important as the language of the heart is, in and of itself, it is not yet sufficient, because it must yet be transformed and interpreted into deeds.[22] The heart may then, indeed, call, but our lives

[18] S. Dom. m. 2, 3, 13-14.

[19] Ep. 130, 9, 18.

[20] S. 80,1,2.

[21] En. Ps. 49,23.

[22] En. Ps. 125,8.

must call as well. And our lives call primarily through works of righteousness. Augustine interprets the appeal "Our Father, who art in Heaven" as "Our Father, who dwells in the hearts of the righteous as in his holy temple". "Someone who prays, must, at the same time, desire that the one to whom he or she appeals dwells within him- or herself. If the person eagerly strives to that end, he or she must also practice righteousness, because by this work of love, he or she invites God to live in his or her heart".[23]

In other texts, Augustine renders his understanding of righteousness in clear terms. He describes righteousness as obeying God's law. Only if the praying person turns steadfastly toward God's law is God's ear steadfastly directed toward him.[24] No one can praise God, unless there is agreement between words and deeds; here, deeds mean love of God and one's neighbor. It makes no sense to call with our voices and remain dumb in our deeds. Calling to Christ is therefore the same as responding to Christ's grace with good deeds. Good deeds are: forsaking worldly pleasures, giving to the poor and the needy, paying no attention to insults, taking no vengeance, praying for your enemies.[25] In this context, prayer has two wings: saving money by fasting, and giving money to feed the poor. It is on these wings that our prayers ascend to God.[26] Due to the fact that the drum and the psaltery are two musical instruments that are played with the hands, Augustine explains the psalm verse: "Let them sing a psalm for God with drum and psaltery" by referring to Matthew 25: 32-46:

> "Why does the psalmist say: I take up a drum or a psaltery? In order to praise God not only with the voice but with actions as well...It is the same for you if, when you sing alleluia, you also hand out bread to the hungry, clothe the naked, and welcome the stranger. Then it is not only your voice that makes a sweet sound but your hands too are joining in, because your deeds are in tune with your words". [27]

[23] S. dom. M. 2,5,18.
[24] En. Ps. 85,10.
[25] S. 33,5,5 and s. 88,13,12.
[26] En. Ps. 42,8.
[27] En. Ps. 149,8.

2. The Position during Prayer

Naturally, Augustine is familiar with the various physical postures that were common in liturgical prayer. But, due to his great emphasis upon the internal posture when praying, the external is given little attention.

When they pray, the faithful stand facing East, where the sun rises. Standing facing the sun is, for Augustine, a symbol of our devotion to God, who surpasses the entire cosmos.[28] Standing erect while praying is a sign of the Resurrection.[29]

Beating the breast is a confession of guilt, by means of which we lament the more hidden sins in our hearts. In any case, we sin, not only in external deeds, but also in the inner recesses of our hearts, which remain hidden from other human beings. Before God, however, they do not remain hidden, and for this reason this confession is directed first and foremost toward God. Augustine calls beating the breast: "castigating his hidden sins with an external sign".[30]

Then we find praying on one's knees, praying stretched out on the ground (prostration), praying with bowed head.[31] We can pray with our facial expression; we can pray with rejoicing or with tears.[32] Just as Abel's blood has a voice that calls out to God from the ground (Genesis 4:10), so, too, do tears have a voice, because tears are the heart's blood. Therefore, offer your hearts, your inner blood, to God.[33]

Even the eyes play a certain role. Although normally, the tongue speaks, in a certain sense, the speech of the eyes interprets the longing that is present in prayer: "In what way do eyes ask: 'When will you comfort me?' Only if you pray and seek with this purpose and expectation! Normally the tongue speaks, and the

[28] S. Dom. m. 2,5,18.
[29] Ep. 55,15,28.
[30] S. 67,1.
[31] En. Ps. 140,18.
[32] S. Mai 15,1.
[33] S. Morin 16,7.

eyes do not. But the longing of prayer is, in a certain sense, the voice of the eyes".[34]

Praying to God with uplifted hands maintains a connection to Christ's outstretched hands on the Cross, with keeping God's Commandments, and with good works. The connection between outstretched hands and the doing of deeds of love is not so strange if we consider that even now the expression "reach out your hands to the poor" is common. "On the Cross, the Lord lifted up his hands for our sake. His hands were outstretched on the Cross for our sake. His hands were outstretched on the Cross so that our hands should be outstretched to do good works. His Cross brought us mercy... Let us lift up our hands to God in prayer as well. We shall not stand ashamed with our hands uplifted to God if we exercise them in good works... Why is it required that we pray to God with uplifted hands? The Apostle says, in any case: 'Uplifted, clean hands, without anger or strife' (1 Timothy 2:8). So that whenever you lift up your hands to God, your works may come to mind". [35] Moses, who prays with uplifted arms against the threat that comes from Amalek (Exodus 17:8-16), is a prefiguration of Jesus, who conquers evil on the Cross.[36] Whenever we see someone in prayer with outstretched hands, we recognize the Cross. It seems to have been the custom in North Africa for some people to apply a visible sign of the Cross to the forehead. This is done because one desires to honour a ridiculed symbol and proclaim the splendor of a despised symbol. Against this background, we understand the following text:

> "Many apply the sign of the Cross to their foreheads without concerning themselves with the significance of doing so. God wants performers of this symbol, not painters. If you wear the sign of Christ's humility on your foreheads, wear it in your hearts as well, and emulate Christ's humility".[37]

[34] En. 20,2 Ps. 118.
[35] En. Ps. 62,13-14. En. Ps. 87,9. Io. eu. tr. 118,5. En. 114,4 Ps. 118.
[36] Trin. 4,15,20. S. 352,2,6.
[37] S. 32,13,13.

Augustine relates how his mother, Monnica, chided one of his disciples, Licentius, because he sat in the privy, singing the psalm verse "God of might, turn to us; show your face and we shall be saved" (Psalm 80:8). But Licentius answered her: "As if God would not hear my voice if some foe or other held me captive here".[38]

External postures are for Augustine gestures that show something of our inner will and orientation. God does not need the signs, but for ourselves, they are a stimulus to pray and beg for help more humbly and with greater fervor. I do not know, Augustine says, how these external bodily postures cause our inner emotions to increase, but they do cause the heart's affection to grow, the affection, which was, actually, the precursor of the external. But if, for one reason or another, a person cannot assume these positions, that is not to say that someone cannot pray inwardly and lie prostrate before the eyes of God.[39] Once Simplicianus asked Augustine the question how he was to understand the text "King David went into the sanctuary and sat down in the presence of the Lord" (2 Samuel 7:18). After citing various examples from the Bible that speak of sitting in the presence of God (Elijah in 1 Kings 18:42), standing in God's presence (the tax collector in Luke 18:13), kneeling before God (Acts 7:60. 20:36), lying in bed and there praying (Psalm 6:7), Augustine concludes:

> "There exists no prescription concerning the position of the body during prayer. The most important thing is that our mind is present to God and experiences its being turned to God...When a person wants to pray, he adopts that attitude which is best fit to move the mind... If the desire to pray comes suddenly, we should not postpone praying because we wish first to seek a place where we can retire, where we can pray standing up or prostrating. The concentration of the mind creates a kind of solitude for itself".[40]

[38] Ord. 1,8,22.
[39] Cur. mort. 5,7.
[40] Simpl. 2, q. 4.

V. The Many Forms of the Prayer of Praise

1. Worshipping God

Before we discuss the various ways of praying in the case of Augustine[1], we must consider his thoughts regarding the worshipping of God. He is not familiar with the worship or adoration of God as a special exercise in prayer, as later became the fashion. His view of adoration has its foundations quite entirely in the text: "You shall worship no other gods but me, for I am the Lord, your God" (Exodus 20:5, Deuteronomy 6:13, Matthew 4:10). Worshipping God is thus tantamount to serving and honoring the one true God. We can also express it in these terms: worshipping God is tantamount to believing in the one personal God of the Bible. Worshipping him, and throwing oneself down on one's knees for him is contrasted with believing in false gods and honoring some form or other of created reality. We are permitted to worship only the Maker of Creation; no angel, no human being, no martyr, no heavenly body, such as the sun, or the moon.[2] Augustine draws a distinction between "honoring" and "venerating." "Venerating" has the meaning "worshipping." "Honoring" has a more general meaning. "Everyone who worships, honors. But someone who honors does not yet worship". We can and must honor human beings, but we must not worship them. If we honor a righteous human being, we do so to follow his or her example, not to worship him or her. We honor him or her in love, not in total servitude or submission.[3] For the unique worship or veneration of God, Augustine prefers to use the Greek word, *latreia,* (serving God – as opposed to idolatry), because the human being owes service, in the strict sense, only to God.[4]

[1] We spoke already about the short prayer.
[2] Io. eu. tr. 13,2. S. 46,8,17. S. 319,1,1. En. Ps. 93,4.
[3] C. s. Arrian. 23,19. Vera rel. 55,108-113.
[4] Trin. 1,6,13. Ciu. 10,1,2-3. 19,17.

For this reason, Augustine regards worship as the basis of all praying. Worship is, as it were, the soil in which the many forms of prayer may fully blossom. He will then also say: "Praying is one thing; worshipping is another thing". In this context, he gives a sensitive interpretation of 1 Timothy 2:1 "Before all else, I admonish you to perform supplications *(deprecationes)*, prayers *(orationes)*, intercessions *(interpellationes)*, and prayers of thanksgiving *(gratiarum actiones)* in the presence of all people". Taking the original Greek text of this passage as a point of departure, he then provides an interpretation of its most important words. To supplicate *(precari)* is to ask for good things, but beseeching *(deprecari)* is asking to avert evil. In the case of the word "prayers *(orationes)*", he protests against some Latin translations that have the word "adoration *(adorationes)*". "Adoring" is usually an improper translation. According to the Greek, what is at issue is prayer as a unity of desire and faith, because in prayer, the human being dedicates him- or herself to Christ; one promises to remain in Christ. Augustine links "intercessions *(interpellationes)*" with "Christ, who speaks most effectively on our behalf" (Romans 8:34), who appeals, as our intercessor, on our behalf, to the most merciful power of God. We, too, must be intercessors for all human beings. Finally, there is the prayer of thanksgiving, which Augustine does not address further. He applies this plan to the celebration of the Eucharist, which begins with prayers to avert evil, after which the solemn prayer of the consecration, up to and including the Our Father follows, then the intercessions on the part of the bishop to beseech God's blessing upon the faithful, to conclude with the prayer of thanksgiving.[5] In this text, in which he brands adoration as a mistranslation, it becomes clear that worshipping is actually the foundation of the many different forms of praying. Many other texts bear this out. It is on the basis of our worship of God that we can confess our guilt and our thanks in his presence, that we can beseech him and weep in his presence, appeal to him, and ask him for help, glorify him and thank him.[6]

[5] S. 149,2,12-16.

[6] See a. o. S. 176,5,5 and S. 216,9,9. En. Ps. 85,13 and En. Ps. 131,24.

As is apparent, from the Bible Augustine knows many ways of praying. The most commonly occurring are the prayer of praise and the prayer of supplication. But, between these two, there are many degrees of distinction that we should try to describe. We begin with the prayer of praise, because, for Augustine, this is the most exalted form of praying: "Praising God is the most exalted work of human beings. It is God's work to please you through his beauty. It is your work to praise him with thanksgiving".[7]

2. Praising God

The fact that we can praise God is a gift that he himself gave us.[8] For Augustine, there are three ways in which we can praise God: with our voices, with our hearts, and with our lives. In addition, there are many reasons for praising God. We find them in Creation, in the fact that we exist, in God's acts of salvation for the chosen Jewish people, we find them in righteousness as a result of the grace of Jesus Christ. Thus, we must, in the final analysis, praise God in everything.[9] Though God is unspeakable, and though we can never quite express the experience of our faith in words, we are not, however, permitted to be silent. We must praise him and give him thanks. We owe him adoration, respect, and praise.[10] We cannot see God, but we can, indeed, look at his works. The created world is already, for the believer, good reason to praise God. An incomparably stronger impetus is his incarnated son, Jesus, in whom God has rendered himself knowable to the most profound degree. But, even after God's revelation in Jesus, we cannot praise God as he is in himself. When Moses asked God: what must I tell the people when they ask your name, he heard, in reply "I am; that is who I am" (Exodus 3:14). Augustine

[7] En. Ps. 44,9 and En. Ps. 72,34.

[8] En. Ps. 62,12.

[9] En. Ps. 134,15. En. Ps. 144,10.

[10] En. Ps. 99,6.

provides the following commentary: we cannot praise God as "I am; that is who I am". But God moderated this praise with something that we can readily understand by immediately adding "I am the God of Abraham, the God of Isaac, and the God of Jacob" (Exodus 3:15). With that, God indicated that he is a God for us.[11] Augustine is well aware of the fact that our daily praise of God is weak and incapable of expressing God's exalted state. Our impotence to praise God as he is must lead us to humility and contribute to directing our thoughts more inwardly, so that we become more receptive of him whom we are praising.[12] We must not think that we can sufficiently praise him whose greatness is without end.[13] At the same time, he issues a warning against people who regard this life as squalor and say that praising God is, for us lowly human beings, an impossible and senseless thing.[14]

3. Praising and Loving

Praising God is linked to faith, hope, and love. The reason is that we carry praise of God in the treasury of our heart. In our heart we carry the faith, hope, and love that God himself has given us. As an offering of praise, we give these back to God.[15] A few times, Augustine forges a link between praising and hoping[16], but by far, most of the texts describe praising as an aspect of love. 'Praise' and 'love' are related to one another. For what is praise? What do we do if we praise something or someone? Does praising not consist of this: recognizing that which is of value in something or

[11] En. Ps. 134,5-6.

[12] En. Ps. 145,6 and 4.

[13] En. Ps. 144,5.

[14] En. Ps. 119,4. I think here on the words of D. Sölle on suffering: "When it is no longer allowed to praise God, and when the opinion prevails that in this absurd life there is no good at all and nothing worth praising, then we get a multiplication of fears of one another".

[15] En. Ps. 50,21. En. Ps. 55,12.

[16] En. Ps. 146,1.

someone, finding approval of that quality, and expressing it in words or gestures? For this reason, only someone who admires a person or thing, can praise. In order to admire a person or thing, one must love. Love is a precondition for being able to praise. Thus, the prayer of praise is an act of love. Augustine says: "But my soul wants to praise you in order to love you. It wants to confess your mercy to you in order to praise you".[17] The confession of God's praise is itself a total sacrifice (*holocaustum*) because it consumes our whole hearts in the fire of love. Whoever approaches God's altar is included in that burnt offering.[18]

In the notion of the confession of God's mercy as praise, one aspect of the prayer of praise comes to the fore that we might not think of directly. We praise God not only by rejoicing in his greatness, which would come under the heading of joy, but also in the confessions of our sins and faults, which rather comes under the heading of sadness and regret. And yet, the confession of one's sins before God entails an aspect of praise.[19] The sinner who has no hope of forgiveness of his or her sins remains shut up in his or her despair. But whoever confesses his or her sins to God acknowledges him as God and Lord. By doing so, the human being proclaims his or her faith in him. But even more, he or she asks for God's goodness and compassion, which means, in itself, praise of God. As an example, Augustine cites the case of a physician: the more the patient thinks that he is incurably ill, the more the physician is praised when the patient recovers.[20] Thus, self-blame on the part of the sinner bears witness to his faith in God as a liberator, and he or she praises God's goodness by means of this witness.[21]

There is no crucial difference between praising God now, in this life, and after this life. The relationship between both may be

[17] Conf. 5,1,1.
[18] En. Ps. 42,5.
[19] En. Ps. 105,2 and En. Ps. 117,1.
[20] En. Ps. 94,4.
[21] S. 67,1,1 – 2,4.

described as a transition from many songs of praise to one single song of praise.[22] The praise of God here on earth is continued in the heavenly joy, because eternal love means eternal praise. "What will our activity entail there? Praising God: loving and praising. Praising in love and loving in songs of praise". "The praise of God will be our activity. Love and you will praise, but you cease praising if you cease loving".[23] But we do not attain eschatological, heavenly praise if we do not devote ourselves to praising God here, in this life: "Because the eternal joy of our life to come will consist of praising God, the preparation of our present lives must consist of the praise of God. No one is comfortable praising God throughout eternity if he or she does not practice doing so in this life. Therefore, let us praise God".[24] Whoever does not wish to praise in this passing world will remain silent when the world without end comes".[25] Here we learn from creation to praise God. The praise of God that puts us on the right path must show us what we love and what we fear, what we choose, and what we reject.[26]

The Our Father begins with an act of praise: "Our Father, who art in heaven". This praise is a sign of love, because normally, the word "father" refers to a loving relationship.[27] Repeatedly, Augustine stresses that we must praise God eagerly and voluntarily. Why? The reason is that we love God in exchange of nothing (*gratis*) and not for the sake of something else: "What I praise, I love for free. I praise God and in that praise, I rejoice". It is not as it is in theatrical plays, in which the playgoers become carried away encouraging and praising a charioteer, a fighter of wild beasts, or a stage actor. If their favorites lose, they feel ashamed. We must not act that way before God. We should praise him altogether out of free will, love and praise him selflessly, without

[22] En. Ps. 144,3.
[23] En. Ps. 147,3. En. Ps.85,24. En. Ps. 83,8.
[24] En. Ps. 148,1.
[25] En. Ps. 144,2.
[26] En. Ps. 144,7-8.
[27] En. Ps. 104,1.

thought for our own benefit.[28] Augustine goes on to say that we do most things out of necessity: build houses, make clothing, make certain that there is food. But there is something that we do purely out of free will, namely loving what we praise. We praise and love God not for this reason, or that, but simply because God pleases us (*placet*). In modern language, the word *placet* is hardly translatable.[29] We might render it as "because I find God good, because I find joy in him". Elsewhere, Augustine says: "Confess God only because doing so is good".[30] We can compare this with two people who love one another; if one asks why they love each other, they cannot say much more than "because it is good". True love does not admit an other response than: it is the beloved person him- or herself.

A direct consequence of this praising of God purely out of free will, without any ulterior motive, is that we have praised him already by wanting to praise him. The will to praise is already praise.We can never say: Indeed, I want to offer something to God, but I have nothing to offer him. Our desire is enough. Thus, we can never say, either: I should want to praise God, but I have nothing. Our desire is enough. Even if we find no words to praise him, it is not so bad, because it is our heart he seeks.[31]

Following from the link between praise and love, there is yet another important consequence. By praising, one appropriates what is praised to a certain degree. "You incorporate it into yourself. If you praise an unrighteous person for the sake of his or her unrighteousness, you, yourself are unrighteous. If you praise a thief, you make yourself an accomplice. But, if you praise a righteous person, then, by virtue of the fact that you praise him or her, you share in his or her righteousness. In any case, you praise no righteous person if you do not love him or her. And you would not love him or her if you derived no benefit from doing

[28] En. Ps. 53,10.
[29] En. Ps. 134,11.
[30] En. Ps. 53,10.
[31] En. Ps. 134,11.

so yourself".[32] The words "if you derived no benefit from doing so" mean that praising yields an advantage to the person who praises. Augustine draws the conclusion from this that it is not the person or thing that is praised, but rather, the person who does the praising who is to be congratulated. Someone who praises the goodness in another person need not be thanked so much, as congratulated, even if he or she were wrong about the other person's goodness. Righteous people congratulate those who praise.[33] Praising the good does not benefit that which is praised, but those who praise.[34] This is not so strange as it might perhaps appear. Praise brings with it not one single advantage for the good that is being praised. A noble thing, or a good person, remain what they are. Their goodness does not increase because they are praised and exalted. But praise does, indeed, enhance the goodness of the person who does the praising, because honest praise always includes longing for the good that is being praised. One desires to pursue this good and to own it oneself. Thus, praise is bearing witness for him or her who praises.

"When good persons are praised, the benefit falls on those who praise, not on those who are praised. For as far as the latter are concerned, it is enough for them that they are good; but the former, whose advantage it is to imitate the good, are to be congratulated when they praise the good because they give evidence that those whom they praise sincerely are pleasing to them".[35]

Thus, through our praise, we do not magnify God, but we, ourselves, become magnified by it. By knowing God and admiring him in awe, I become greater. We add nothing to the glory of God; rather, he makes us holier, happier, and more glorious.[36] "See what an advantage it brings you to praise God". Thus, praise of God becomes, as it were, food for us:

[32] En. Ps. 134,4.
[33] Ep. 20,2. Vera relig. 55,111.
[34] Io. Eu. tr. 100,1.
[35] Ep. 231,4.
[36] En. Ps. 103, s. 1,3; En. Ps. 39,4.

> "Praise his name, for the Lord is sweet. Never think that you will weary of praising him. Your songs of praise are like eating; the more you praise, the more strength you acquire, and the more delightful does he become whom you are praising.".[37]

On the basis of what has been said above, Augustine himself dares turn things around. If we praise God with our words, then we are praised in God, by God's words. They are, indeed, our words, but we received them from God. Our words are thus, at the same time, and even first of all, God's words. They come from him and they have become our own. God gave us the words of praise and he wanted them to be from me for the sake of loving him, from whom they came originally. From him they have come for my sake, and they have become my own. Thus, we obtain the praise that we give God; we get it back, also from him, when we are praised in God.[38] By praising God, we praise ourselves, at least if we are not arrogant and recognize that all the good in us comes from him:

> "Among all the things God, who made them, made also you. It seems to follow, then, that if you praise God's works you will have to praise yourself, since you are a work of God".[39]

"Being praised in God" means that we cannot strive "to be praised for our own sakes". Only the haughty want to be praised for their own sakes. In this context, Augustine uses the concrete image of the donkey on which the Lord sat as he entered Jerusalem (Mark 11:1-11). Just like the donkey, we, too, carry Christ. But it was not the donkey that was praised, but rather, the Lord. Thus, we can demand no praise for ourselves, because then we would more nearly resemble rearing horses, unwilling to work, but not the lowly, gentle donkeys.[40]

37 En. Ps. 99,17.
38 En. Ps. 55,7.
39 En. Ps. 144,7.
40 En. 2 Ps. 33, 5.

4. Praising and Living

Praising God must not remain limited to within the church building. Augustine warns his faithful not to think that when they leave the church and go home, that the business of praising God is finished. We must always praise God by living well. If we never cease living well, we praise God without interruption. But, if we deviate from God's will, and from righteousness, we cease praising God. Our tongues may be silent, but our lives must call out. If we live in such a way that it is a praise of God, then, such a life is, in fact, a response to God's calling, not with the tongue alone, but with life itself.[41] And if we make the transition to other activities, we must continue to praise. It all comes down to the fact that we praise God in all the actions of our daily lives: in doing business, in eating and drinking, in child-rearing, in our rest and sleep. In all things, we can praise God by enjoying, in gratitude, what he has created.

"Do not let your heart be dumb or your life silent. You are singing and playing psalms to God, if you have no truck with fraud in your business. Praise God when you are eating and drinking... If you eat and drink moderately, frugally, and temporately... even your food and drink are praise offered to God... After you have eaten and drunk, you retire to sleep. Do not do anything unseemly in bed or go beyond what God's law permits you. Let the bed you share with your spouse be chaste. If you are trying to procreate children, keep your sexual pleasure within bounds. Be considerate toward your spouse in bed, for both of you are members of Christ, both are created by him, and both are re-created by his blood... If you conduct yourself like this you are praising God and there is no question of the praise you offer him being interrupted".[42]

Praising God by singing Alleluia is not something you always do with your voices; indeed, it is always possible to do so with

[41] En. Ps. 148,2. En. 2 Ps. 101, 6.
[42] En. Ps. 146,1-2.

your hearts. In any case, our hearts encompass our whole lives and all our deeds. Let us therefore praise God with our lives and our tongues, with our hearts and mouths, with our voices and our noble behavior.[43]

We have seen how Augustine interprets "hands" as a symbol of good works. "Clap your hands for God" means: do good works.[44] Good works are altogether concrete. God says: I am with you if, with a good heart, you give bread to the hungry. In this regard, Augustine uses the symbol of psaltery and cither in the sense of physical works. Playing the ten-stringed psaltery in praise of God is keeping God's commandments. Our deeds are our psaltery, because everyone who does good deeds with his or her hands, plays the psaltery and cither for God. Our work is our psaltery.[45] Whoever lives for God, sings for God. Whoever works for the glory of God, plays the psaltery for his name's sake.[46] The sound of the psaltery is made in the uppermost portion of the instrument. The sound of the cither, by contrast, is made in the bottom-most portion. Playing the psaltery means, therefore, praising God for his higher gifts, especially for the ten strings that are the symbol of the ten commandments. Playing the cither means praising God for his earthly goods, both in good times and bad.[47]

Ultimately, praising with our lives amounts to this: we, ourselves, must be God's praise. The singer himself is the praise of God, which is being sung. And we are the praise, if we live well. Whoever lives badly does not praise God.[48] The human being who turns back toward him-or herself finds there what he or she must offer. Within ourselves, we find the sacrifice of praise we want to make. If we are a good offering of praise, it is because

[43] En. Ps. 106,1. S. 256,1.

[44] En. Ps. 46,3.

[45] En. Ps. 42,8; En. Ps. 91,3.

[46] En. Ps. 67,5; En. Ps. 104,2.

[47] En. 2 Ps. 32, s.1,5-6; En. Ps. 42,5 and 8; En. 2 Ps 70, 11; En. Ps.104,2; En. Ps. 143,16.

[48] S. 34,3,6.

God has given it to us, and we must thank God for all the good that is in us.[49] In this way, we praise God in ourselves. In fact, we are, and we show, God's power and greatness because he has given us all that as a gift. We, ourselves, are his rejoicing trumpet, his psaltery, cither, tympany, choir, strings, organ, and cymbal.[50]

5. God Praises Himself

"I would go so far as to say to you, beloved, that God has praised himself in order to give human beings a pattern by which they can praise him in a seemly fashion. Because God has kindly praised himself, men and women know how to praise him. It cannot, of course, be said to God, as it is to humans: Let not your own mouth praise you (Prov. 27:2). If a human being praises himself, it is arrogance; but if God praises himself, he does so out of his mercy. It is to our advantage to love him whom we praise because by loving the good we become better. Knowing that it is good for us to love him, God has made himself lovable by praising himself, and in making himself knowable he has our good at heart. He therefore stirs up our hearts to praise him, and he has filled his servants with his own Spirit, to enable them to offer him praise. And if it is his own Spirit, present in his servants, who is praising him, what else can we conclude but that God is praising himself".[51]

In the praise of God, also, we find the well-known theme that God goes first, and we follow. It is God's work to please us through his exalted beauty; it is our work to praise him in thanksgiving. By doing that, we return to God what is his.[52] Thanks to the self-revelation and selflessness of God, we can praise him. Our praise is thus a gift from God:

[49] En. Ps. 49,21 and 30.
[50] En. Ps. 150,8.
[51] En. Ps. 144,1.
[52] En. Ps. 44,9.

> "My lips would not praise you, if your mercy did not precede us. I praise you through your gift, I praise you through your mercy. I would not have been able to praise God, if he had not given to me the capability to praise him".[53]

It is the Spirit of God that allows us to discover his lovable nature. But, in most cases, this occurs by way of the goodness of Creation. Creation causes the praise of God to be born. From amazement at the world, praise opens up and blooms:

> "God, the very one who every year makes wine from water, made wine on that day in Cana at a wedding in those six water jars... But it does not amaze us because it happens every year. By its regularity it has lost its wonderment. Yet it merits even greater reflection than that which was done in the water jars. For who is there who reflects upon the works of God, by which the whole world is governed and managed, and is not struck dumb and overwhelmed by miracles? If the human being should reflect on the power of one grain of any seed at all, it is a great thing, an awe, to the one reflecting upon it. But because human beings, concentrating on something else, have abandoned reflection upon the works of God in which they might give praise to the creator every day, God has, therefore, saved for himself, as it were, certain extraordinary things to do so that by amazing events he might arouse human beings, as if they were asleep, to worship him. A dead man arose, human beings were astonished. Every day many are born and no one is amazed".[54]

In many texts, Augustine sings the praises of the beauty and goodness of Creation. Then he usually rises up from the good things of the earth, from what we see of the cosmos, subsequently, via the human body and spirit of humankind, to arrive at God. Gold and silver, the animals and the trees, the charming landscapes that we find on earth, are good. The sun, the moon, and the stars in the heavens are good. You love them. And wherever you love, you praise as well. But do not forget yourselves, because human beings climb above these. Even in your own minds, you read something

[53] En. Ps. 62,12.

[54] Io. Ev. Tr. 8,1.

fascinating, something praiseworthy, and lovable, something that is worth the effort of being longed for and sought after: a certain glistening that you cannot quite hold onto permanently.[55] "In the great book of nature you read the tracks of the Creator".[56] "In the book of your own inner lives you read a reference to God that is clearer by far".[57]

It is thus to human beings that Augustine comes when he talks of praising God through Creation. To be sure, he cites the beauty of the creatures, "their confession", "their voice", "their call", but not without human beings! A stone, a tree, or an animal do not speak or call. Nor can they ask any questions: "The animals, great and small, do, indeed, see the beauty of Creation, but they cannot ask any questions because they have no ordering reason above the messages from their senses. Human beings, however, can ask questions. By virtue of that fact, they can grasp and regard God's invisible mysteries through the created things".[58] The created things themselves cannot praise God directly; they require the mediation of the human intellect and voice. Human beings are the interpreters of Creation; they give voice and heart to all of Creation. The person who looks at things and sees their beauty praises God in everything. When people confess that everything is God's work, they praise God's power, goodness, and greatness. Creation, with heaven and earth, with the sea and everything that moves within it, is the true wealth, even of the poor person, and Creation praises God through us.[59] Augustine sums up his thoughts powerfully at the end of his *Confessions:*

> "Your works praise you so that we love you. And we love you so that your works praise you".[60]

[55] En. Ps. 68, s. 1,5. Conf. 10,6,8-27,38. Io. Ev. Tr. 8,2. About the goodness of creation see also Civ. 5,11 and 22,24.

[56] C. Faust. 32,20.

[57] En. Ps. 145,5. Conf. 7,13,19-17,23. En. Ps. 41,7.

[58] Conf. 10,6,10.

[59] En. Ps. 144,13-14. En. Ps. 148,9. and 15. En. Ps. 68, s. 1,19. S. 241,2,2.

[60] Conf. 13,33,48.

6. Blessing, Honoring, Glorifying, Highly Praising, Exalting, Clarifying God

There are quite a few words that are closely related to praising, and have more or less the same meaning. As the most prominent among them, we cite: blessing *(benedicere)*, in the sense of praising; honoring *(honorare – honorificare)*, as recognizing, openly and expressly, the goodness of someone or something, in word and deed; glorifying *(glorificare)*, in the sense of assenting to the splendor of the goodness; highly praising *(magnificare)*, in the sense of proclaiming the greatness of someone or something; to elevate *(exaltare)* in the sense of praising the elevated status of something or someone; clarifying *(clarificare)*, in the sense of proclaiming someone's brilliance, luster and glory. We shall not deal with all these words at length. A few references to them will suffice.

Blessing

We usually translate the word "benedicere" as blessing. Blessing then has the meaning: wishing and performing good things for someone. But we cannot do this with regard to God. Where it is a matter of "blessing" God in a liturgical service, we must translate it as "speaking well of God, extolling him, praising him". The other meaning of the word "to bless" is giving away good things. God blesses human beings with good gifts and human beings praise God as the source and beginning of all good. The initiative thus lies with God:

> "The Lord's blessing of us has the priority, and our blessing of the Lord is its consequence. His blessing is like the rain, and our response in blessing him is the fruit".[61]

Here, too, singing praises is prayer par excellence. The fact that we must never cease, inwardly, to bless God, is, for Augustine, tantamount to the appeal: our soul must praise God always. Blessing God in the sense of praising God occurs only where God's will is

[61] En. Ps. 66,1.

done and where a good life is led. For hearing and not doing is building on sand. And if God causes good things to happen through me and in me, the good things are actually God's works, which "bless" him, that is to say, praise him. It is not our merit.[62]

Honoring

In conjunction with honoring God, Augustine brings the same thought to the fore that we encountered in praising God. In response to the question: "What shall I offer God?", Augustine replies with God's words from psalm 50:23: "An offering of praise will do me honor".[63] Of course, we must remain aware of the fact that our honoring of God can never be equal to the exalted position of God, which surpasses everything. Our words will always fall short of the mark. Publicly proclaiming God's works is to bring him a deed of honor, but, in his presence, respectful silence is more appropriate than any human word.[64] "One honors nothing unless one loves it".[65] Even the fact that we find the good good, and that we desire the good, that we honor God and accept Christ, are gifts from God. The fact that God is honored by someone who lives in a holy way, is a grace from God.[66] If we honor that in ourselves which is from God, then we, who are created by God, will be honored in God. But if we honor that in ourselves which is from God as something that is from us and not from God, we are far removed from the Holy One.[67] The fact that human beings honor one another is something good. For where human beings honor one another, they praise God. Through his power and awe-inspiring transcendence, God created, and he showed these qualities in human beings.[68] The striving for unity

[62] En. Ps. 102, 2 and 28-29. En. 2 Ps. 25, 14.
[63] En. Ps. 53,10.
[64] Ep. 238,4. C. Adim. 11.
[65] En. Ps. 77,20.
[66] Persev. 19,50. Nat. et gr. 63,75.
[67] En. Ps. 55,7.
[68] En. Ps. 150,8.

with the departed Donatists, who are, after all, our brothers, serves just one goal, namely that the Lord's name be honored. Loving unity among human beings means honoring God.[69] It is not for naught that Augustine's Rule says:"And honor God in one another".

Glorifying (glorificare)

Augustine says that the three verbs "glorify (*glorificare*)", "honor (*honorare*)", and "clarify (*clarificare*)" form one reality.[70] Indeed, the terms are related to one another and the difference between them is very subtle.

Augustine reports that before his time, "glory" was defined as follows: "The generally widespread good reputation concerning someone, combined with praise". We praise a human being, because we believe in his good name. Believing, however, is not the same as knowing with certainty. God grows in us the better we know him. For that reason, full knowledge of God is tantamount to the highest glorification of God.[71] In the case of the notion of proclaiming God's glory, we find virtually the same applications we encountered in the case of praising God. We should be God's glory. God's glory dwells within us. Those who belong to the splendour of God's house, in which his glory dwells, are the dwelling place of God's glory.[72] But our exaltation of God cannot enhance his glory, for the glory that he possesses in himself always remains the same. Precisely by giving his glory to us does he impart greater glory and honor to us. What do we do, then, when we exalt God? We proclaim his glory aloud, but we do not create his glory.[73] When Augustine talks about Matthew 5:16 "Your light must shine before the eyes of the people, so that they see your good works and exalt your Father,

[69] S. 357,4.
[70] C. s. Arrian. 31,29.
[71] S. Guelf. 22,5. Io. Ev. Tr. 105,3.
[72] En. 2 Ps. 25,12.
[73] En. Ps. 39,4.

who is in Heaven", he warns his faithful not to become irritated because all exaltation goes toward God. He advises them to be with God, because then they will be exalted in him. To the degree that people humble themselves and desire to be exalted only in him, God becomes more exalted, and they become greater in him.[74] God's glory is our glory.[75] Following the teaching of the text "Do you not know that your body is a temple of the Holy Spirit, who lives in you, and whom you have received from God?... Then exalt God in your body" (1 Corinthians 6: 19-20), Augustine draws the conclusion that the bodies of the faithful are sacrifices for God. For that reason, they should keep their bodies unsullied and free of sin. Our glory rests on the witness of our good conscience (2 Corinthians 1:12).[76]

As reasons why we should exalt God in our bodies, he lists: a) not only our souls, but our bodies, too, are blessed by baptism; b) because our bodies are intended for future immortality. There is thus also future glory for our bodies, stored up with God.[77] Not only are we saved in God, we are also clothed in glory. Our righteousness is part of our salvation; our exaltation is part of the honor that is given to us.[78]

Highly Praising (magnificare)

Augustine's *Confessions* begin with the words: "Great you are, Lord, and very praiseworthy". God's greatness is apparent from the fact that he has done great things in the history of salvation. In addition, he should be praised as the Creator of all great things that we encounter in the world. God is always great because his greatness is eternally the same. But his greatness is not seen and recognized by all people:

[74] S. Guelf. 22,5.
[75] S. 47,9,13. S. 380,6.
[76] C. Max. 2,21,1. Ep. 173A,10. S. 185,3,3.
[77] Nupt. et conc. 1,18,20. En. 2 Ps. 101,14.
[78] En. Ps. 61,13.

> "I did not understand you before... but now I understand you to be great. You are great always, even when you are hidden, but you became great for me when you revealed yourself. In this sense you have been magnified through me... I am not marveling at something that has become great from the time I learned about it. I marvel because I have become great myself since I learned... He has become magnified exceedingly in the works he performs in our regard".[79]

This text is rather complicated. Fortunately, Augustine clarifies his words by referring to the prayer of the Our Father "Hallowed be thy name". God is always holy and we cannot enhance his holiness. It is thus a question of our sanctification, namely that we keep the name of God holy. The same holds true of the words: "You have become great through me". The significance of this is tantamount to: as a result of God's greatness, which he brings about in me (and in us), the divine greatness is praised. His greatness is apparent from the greatness that God gives to human beings. Thus, Paul, too, says: "And they praised God's greatness in me" (Galatians 1:24).[80] We ought to expect, at this juncture, that Augustine would refer to Mary's *Magnificat:* "My soul greatly praises the Lord" (Luke 1:46), but he makes the connection, rather, with Mary in the text of Matthew 12:50: My mother is she who does my Father's will. "The Lord greatly praised in Mary the fact that she did the will of the Father".[81] This is in keeping with Augustine's approach to Mary, whom he usually represents as a model of faith and as the first of the faithful. Nor is it so surprising that Augustine has the Lord praise Mary greatly, because he keeps emphasizing God's initiative.

It is our confession of God's name that makes us great. All those who become blessed in Christ (of whom Abraham was the prefiguration) will praise him greatly. We do not make God great, and yet we do something for him by praising him and proclaiming his

[79] En. 1 Ps. 103,3.
[80] S. 149,13,14.
[81] Io. Ev. Tr. 10,3.

greatness.[82] Lauding God greatly in praise is my greatest wealth, says Augustine. And there are several reasons for confessing God's greatness at all times. God did not merely call us to himself and inspire us to confess our sins to obtain forgiveness, he also gave us the gift of living well. He must be highly praised because he leads us and because – if we persevere to the end – he glorifies us.[83] But Augustine is not merely thinking of himself here; he worries about his departed brethren, the Donatists. I do not want to be alone to praise God highly, he says, I do not want to be alone to love him; I do not want to be alone to embrace him. Elsewhere the bishop has said to his people: I don't want to be saved without you.[84]

Exalting (exaltare)

"Exaltation," too, is one of the many aspects of praising. Exalting God means confessing his high and exalted status, and praising him. Here, too, it holds true that we can add nothing to God's exalted status, but that singing his high praises benefits us.[85] Here, Augustine takes Christ as an example, as intermediary become human, he intercedes between God and us on our behalf.

"Accordingly you must understand that it is not illogical for him who became a human being for your sake to pray for you. And if it is not illogical for him to pray for you, he could quite reasonably say these words also on your behalf: I will exalt you, Lord, because you have taken me up (Ps. 30:1)".[86]

Exalting God has to do not only with God's exalted status, but also with his compassion. If we are humbly mindful of the compassionate God, we shall be worthy of enjoying his exalted status. To this end, it is necessary that we not exalt ourselves, but find our glory in the Lord.[87] Exalting God in truth and in a correct way

[82] En. Ps. 19,6. En. Ps. 71,19.
[83] En. 2 Ps. 68,15. En. Ps. 69,6.
[84] En. 2 Ps. 33,6. S. 17,2,6.
[85] En. Ps. 106,13. S. 380,6.
[86] En. 2 Ps. 29,4.
[87] En. Ps. 41,12.

consists of exalting him who made us righteous. He created the righteousness, which we possess and which is present in us. In us, he will crown not our merits, but his gifts. For that reason, we must praise him highly.[88] We do, indeed, praise God's exalted status with our tongues, but that is not enough. We should also do that with our hearts and our lives. That is how Augustine understands the particular translation of Psalm 66:17 that he had before him. In a modern translation, this verse says: "My appeal to him had hardly gone out, or a song of praise lay on my lips", but in Augustine's, it says: "I called to him with my mouth, and I exalted him under my tongue". Over against publicly proclaiming God's exalted status, he places the confession of the exalted status in the realm of the hidden. Augustine makes here a distinction between proclaiming and confessing. The expression "under the tongue" refers, according to him, to silent consideration, and to the human heart.[89] With respect to the concrete life of every day, it is important that human beings maintain unity with one another. Without unity, there can be no response to God's elevated status. Therefore, Augustine appeals to the Donatists, to exalt God's name in unity.[90]

Proclaiming God's Splendor (clarificare)

"By splendor, someone can become illustrious, and by being illustrious, exalted". Giving splendor is the same thing as glorifying, says Augustine, with reference to John 17: 1, where it is said, in relation to Jesus' resurrection: "Glorify the Son so that the Son might glorify you". Because God's splendor cannot be increased or diminished, the goal of this text is to acquaint the world with God's splendor by proclaiming Jesus' resurrection.[91] The nature of God is splendor. He is an unspeakable light. Therefore, God's splendor is always the same, and never changing; thus, the change

[88] En. Ps. 98,8.
[89] En. Ps. 65,21.
[90] En. 2 Ps. 33,7.
[91] Io. Ev. Tr. 100,1. 104,3. 105,1.

comes from our side.[92] It has to do with the fact that the name of our Lord, Jesus Christ becomes splendid in us and we become splendid in him, as we read in 2 Thessalonians 1:12. The word *claritas* can also be translated as "brightness, radiance, shimmering, brilliance". In the account of Jesus' transfiguration, it says that "Jesus' face began to shine like the sun" (Matthew 17:2). Augustine interprets this as "the shining of the Gospel", because the grace of Jesus' good news shines throughout the world.[93] When we pray: "Show your splendor to the eyes of all peoples, as you have shown your splendor in us" (Sir. 36:4), we are saying nothing more than the Our Father "Hallowed be thy name".[94] It is thus our job to be the radiation of God's splendor. We find this attractively stated in the following text:

> "We love the beauty of the house of the Lord, and the place of the tent of his glory, if that is what we are ourselves... For the temple of God is holy, which you are (1 Cor. 3:17)...When the hearts of the faithful, as living stones (1 Pt. 2:5), are cemented together with the bond of love, it constitutes the beauty of God's house and the place of the tent of his glory".[95]

It comes as no surprise to us that in this context, Augustine appeals to the Scriptural text: "Those who allow my lustre to shine shall I make lustrous" (1 Samuel 2:30). With these words, he addresses himself to the Donatists, who do not wish to recognize God's salvation as intended for the whole world. [96]

7. Jubilation and Shouting with Joy

Being jubilant is a particular form of praising. When words fall short of the mark, we sometimes resort to making inarticulate

[92] En. Ps. 109,12.
[93] S. 79.
[94] Ep. 130,12,22.
[95] S. 15,1,1.
[96] C. ep. Parm. 2,19,38.

sounds of joy. Being joyful presupposes our inability to comprehend and to express in words what is singing in our hearts. That occurs primarily in conjunction with very great joy or in the case of a joy that is so intense that it cannot be expressed in words. Here Augustine cites the examples of workers who sing while they work. When the human language finds it so difficult to praise creatures that were created by God, what is left for us than to shout before the Creator? An overwhelming and inexpressible joy, that is the sacrifice of our jubilation. Where there is no joy, there is no jubilation, either.[97] When directed to an unintelligible and inexpressible God, jubilation is most appropriate:

> "Do not worry, for God provides you with a technique for singing. Do not look after words, as though you could spell out in words anything that will give God pleasure. Sing to him in jubilation. That is what acceptable singing to God means: to sing jubilantly. But what is that? It is to grasp the fact that what is sung in the heart cannot be articulated in words. Think of people who sing at harvest time, or in the vineyard, or during any toil, and leave aside the syllables of the words and switch over to shouts of joy. Even if they begin singing with words and shouts of joy, after a while they seem so full of gladness that they find words no longer adequate to express their feelings. Jubilation is a shout of joy, indicating that the heart is bringing forth something that cannot be expressed in words".[98]

We cannot express God's goodness, and yet, we are not permitted to remain silent. "Woe to those who remain silent concerning you, for with their great prating, they are dumb".[99] But how can we, at one and the same time, not speak and not be silent? Is this not a complete contradiction? Augustine replies: that is possible only by rejoicing with the unspeakable voice of our joy.[100]

[97] En. 2 Ps. 26,12. En. Ps. 99,8.
[98] En. 2 Ps. 32, s. 1, 8.
[99] Conf. 1,4,4.
[100] En. Ps. 102,8.

"There is a saying in another psalm (Ps. 89:16): Blessed the people that understands how to shout with joy. It must be something important, if the understanding of it confers blessing on us… Let us run toward this beatitude. Let us understand why we must shout in joy and let us not burst into witless noise. What would be the use of the shouting for joy and obeying the injunction of the psalm: Shout with joy to God, all the earth, if we did not understand? What would be the point of our voice shouting on its own, if our heart did not? The heart's cry of joy is its understanding… A person who is shouting with gladness does not bother to articulate words. The shout is a wordless sound of joy. It is the cry of a mind expanded with gladness, expressing its feelings as best it can rather than comprehending the sense. When someone is exulting and happy he passes beyond words that can be spoken and understood, and bursts forth into a wordless cry of exultation. Such a person is clearly rejoicing vocally, but he is so full of intense joy that he is unable to explain what makes him happy".[101]

Rejoicing is frequently linked with exulting (*exsultare*). Perhaps exulting is more monotonous than rejoicing, but, like the Bible, Augustine links the two words to one another. The agreement between rejoicing and exultation is that both occur without uttering precisely intelligible words. The word *exsultare* means "leaping up out of joy, being delivered of happiness". The significance of "leaping up" appears when Augustine interprets the text of psalm 84:3 "My heart and my flesh leapt up toward the living God". Here, in the world of temptation, they leapt up rejoicing to the other place of joy. And from where else does that rejoicing upward leaping come from but hope? Toward what are they leaping? Toward the living God. Then Augustine compares the faithful to birds. We, too, fly from our earthly nest toward our heavenly home.[102]

Rejoicing is always associated with joy, especially with the joy of hope. But now, in this life, in most cases, our jubilation is drowned out by entreaties and complaints of woe. In this sense,

[101] En. Ps. 99,3-4.
[102] En. Ps. 83,7.

Augustine distinguishes rejoicing from the prayer of supplication.[103] Our rejoicing is now directed altogether at the eternal rejoicing, because in the life to come, it will be perfect and everlasting.[104] This does not prevent us from having to sing God's praises with great rejoicing here on earth. In praise we rejoice for all creation, for the earth, with its clouds, wind, and rain, for the deliverance of God's people out of slavery.[105]

Our rejoicing, however, should be pure, that is to say: it must be directed toward God, because rejoicing for the Lord differs from rejoicing for banal things. One can, indeed, also rejoice for bad things, which must be rejected without further ado. One can also rejoice for things that are not worth it. How many people are sitting rejoicing in the theater or the circus, at games of all sorts, or in the marketplaces? That is superficial and outer happiness. The faithful should be happy inwardly, in their hearts.[106] Another danger resides in the fact that we direct our rejoicing toward ourselves, and not toward God. It is not for nothing that psalm 2:11 says: "Serve the Lord with awe, and shout with joy for him with trepidation". Thus, we are warned never to rejoice out of self-sufficiency, because that means nothing more than arrogance and pride. We should rejoice before the Lord, through whom we are what we are, and from whom we have received our humanity and our righteousness. The faithful shout of joy "with trepidation", because what they rejoice at arc gifts from God, and not their own merits.[107]

8. Singing and the New Song

Insofar as singing in church is concerned, we see an important development in Augustine's time. As a new convert, he became

103 En. Ps. 99,4. En. Ps. 123,3-4. S. Morin 16,1. En. Ps.54,3.
104 En. Ps. 5,16. En. Ps. 148,1.
105 S. 225,4,4. En. Ps. 134,15.
106 En. Ps. 149,11. En. Ps. 94,2.
107 S. 13,2,2-3,3. Corrept. 9,24.

acquainted with people singing in the church of Ambrose in Milan. Ambrose introduced the Eastern custom of having the people sing the psalm verses. In this way, the faithful participated in a more active way in the liturgical celebrations. In North Africa, Augustine was a great promotor of this innovation. But this new custom also encountered resistance, because some people wanted to adhere to the manner of singing that was customary with Athanasius in Alexandria. There, it more closely resembled reading in a lofty voice, rather than singing. Indeed, Augustine issues a warning against the danger that one can be captivated more by the pleasing voice of the singer than by the text of the song, but he remained a supporter of the innovation nevertheless.

Augustine calls attention to the fact that there are various manners of singing. On the basis of the Holy Scripture, the singing of hymns and psalms can be defended. That serves the purpose of moving the spirit toward piety, and for the purpose of awakening feelings that are full of love. What can Christians who have gathered in church do that would be better, more useful, and holier than to sing, when no readings, no interpretations, or no praying aloud is being done by the bishop? But the customs vary from church to church. The members of the North African Church are rather lazy when it comes to singing in church. That is why the Donatists reproach the Catholics that they sing their psalms too soberly, while they, themselves, sing quite boisterously, as if in a trance.[108] Augustine shows himself to be a supporter of the splendid melodies to which it is customary to sing the psalms. He thinks back upon the deep emotion he experienced in the songs sung in church, shortly after his return to the faith. And yet, he is concerned that the aesthetic enjoyment makes too many demands on his attention, to the detriment of the content of the text. Not incorrectly does he fear that the enjoyment of beauty and true prayer can conflict with one another. Nevertheless, singing in church had to be retained, because as a result of the beauty of the song, our weak minds can be moved all the more readily toward

[108] Ep. 55,18,34-19,35.

love, though they must not be more touched by the singing than by that which was sung.[109]

Psalms are songs that are sung to the accompaniment of the psaltery.[110] A hymn is a song of praise. A hymn must meet three requirements: it must exist for the sake of praising; it must have to do with praising God; and it should be sung.[111] The great wealth of the poor Body of Christ on earth consists in song. The faithful sing with their voices to arouse themselves to praise God. They sing with their hearts to be well pleasing to God. Here, once again, we see the transition from voice to heart, from the external to the internal. Therefore, Augustine calls singing for God our joy, because joy is something internal.[112] There is also a direct link to love because singing is peculiar to a lover. The singer's voice is the ardor of a holy love. Whoever sings God's praises does not merely praise, but also this person praises cheerfully, and loves the one whose praises he sings.[113] Thus, in the case of singing, the law of love applies, namely becoming one with the loved object. In order to do that, it is necessary to understand the content of the song:

> "We want to use our human reason as we sing, not merely to sing like parrots. Blackbirds and parrots and crows and magpies and other species are sometimes taught by people to give voice to words they do not understand. But singing with understanding is restricted to the human being".[114]

In what is sung, one must discover and hear oneself. If we sing already detached from worldly goods, we may be glad to be what we have sung; but if we sing firmly still attached to the earth, then we must wish to become what we have sung.[115] Here, too, Augustine emphasizes the harmony between singing and life, making

[109] Conf. 10,33,50.
[110] En. Ps. 4,1.
[111] En. Ps. 39,4.
[112] En. 2 Ps. 68,15. En. Ps. 147,5.
[113] S. 336,1,1. En. Ps. 72,1.
[114] En. 2 Ps. 18,1.
[115] En. Ps. 38,1.

use of the opposion between what we are and what we have to be. The ten-stringed psaltery is a symbol of the ten Commandments of the Law. Who are the true psalm-singers? Those who do something and do it with joy. On the text "We sang and you did not dance" (Matthew 11:17), we hear the commentary: dancing is a movement of the body that harmonizes with the song. It is the singer who gives an order; the dancer is the one who executes the order. Thus, by living a good life, dancing is agreement with the song.[116] For Augustine, a choir is an image of single-mindedness between human beings. Nearly everyone who lives in a city, he says, knows what a choir is. A choir must have a pleasing sound. If someone sings off-key, it is torture for the ears. Christ's choir is the whole world.[117]

Also in the case of singing, God's gift comes first. For Christ, our hearts and tongues must sing worthy things. But then Christ must deign to give us what we have to sing. No one can sing worthily for him if he has not received from him what he can sing. In point of fact, it is Christ himself who sings in us because we sing as a result of his grace according to the text: "Do you want proof that Christ speaks in me?" (2 Corinthians 13:3).[118] This gift of God, or Christ, has two dimensions: one for this life now, and one for after this life. Now we are en route, as pilgrims. What do wayfarers frequently do? Along the route, they sing. They do not sing because they are enjoying some rest, but as a comfort in their drudgery. They sing, but they keep walking and lighten their tension by singing.

"Now, dear brothers and sisters, let us sing, not to delight in our leisure, but to ease our toil. In the way travelers are in the habit of singing: sing, but keep on walking. Ease your toil by singing, do not fall in love with laziness. Sing, and keep on walking".[119]

[116] En. Ps. 91,5. S. 311,6,6-7,7.
[117] En. Ps. 149,7.
[118] En. 1 Ps. 34,1. Ep. 140,17,44-18,45.
[119] S. 256,3.

Particularly at night wayfarers sing, but then they do so out of fear. They feel themselves surrounded by all sorts of terrifying sounds, or rather, they feel themselves surrounded by a terrifying stillness. The greater the stillness, the more terrifying it is. Sometimes people sing on the road out of fear of robbers. But on the path that is Christ, there is nothing to fear; in Christ, we can sing safely.[120] As pilgrims en route, we must sing with our hearts, that is to say, with longing, because whoever does not experience longing, no matter how much he or she plagues people's ears with their shouts, remains dumb before God.[121] The step from longing in this time to an eschatological interpretation of singing is an obvious one. When the days of singing Alleluia have dawned, Augustine summons his faithful, as good singers, to listen attentively, because what is here is a foretaste of eternal joy.[122] "Sing love songs of your heavenly homeland".[123] In this sense, Augustine interprets the fifteen psalms, which are named "Songs of Ascent" after the fifteen steps of the temple. Nowadays, one speaks of pilgrimage songs. The person who ascends the stairs is the person who ascends with love to the Jerusalem on high. The Psalms of Ascent are the songs of those who burn with a holy longing.[124]

On the basis of various Biblical texts, Augustine frequently speaks about the new song: "Sing a new song to honor Jaweh," (Isaiah 42:10, Psalm 33:3. Apoc. 5:9). He links the new song to Jesus' new commandment: "I give you a new commandment: you must love one another as I have loved you" (John 13:34). Augustine points out that it is actually a very old commandment, because we find it as early as Leviticus 19:18. And yet, the commandment to love one another is new for two reasons: firstly, because it clothes us with the new human being; and secondly, because it is an appeal to love as Christ loved. Not only we, but

[120] En. Ps. 66,6.
[121] En. Ps. 86,1
[122] En. Ps. 110,1.
[123] En. Ps. 66,6.
[124] En. Ps. 126,1.

also the righteous of the Old Testament, are renewed in this way. Together with them we are singers of the new song.[125] For Augustine, new and old are more than indications of time. They have to do with the inner life of the human being, which is either directed toward God, or is not directed toward him. "For what is there that is older than God, who is prior to everything, without end and without beginning. God is new for you when you return to God; by going away from him, you became old".[126] The new song is already old. Christ is eternal, and all those who are renewed in Christ sing the new song. Even the faithful who lived under the Old Testament could be renewed by Christ. However, that does not apply to all, and therefore, Augustine can describe the old song that was sung during the period of the Old Testament as having been directed toward temporal and earthly promises. "In order to sing the new song, it is necessary to love eternal things. That love is new and eternal; it is always new because it does not grow old".[127] But even during the period of the New Testament, there are people who sing an old song. That is the reproach that Augustine addresses to the Donatists, because they sow division in the Church and form a separate Christian community.[128]

The new song is the song of the people who are renewed by grace, and so belong to the New Testament. The New Testament is the Kingdom of Heaven. All our love longs for that kingdom and sings the new song.[129] The old person lives in fear, the new person lives in love. It is thus love that sings the new song. Whoever lives under the law cannot fulfill the law by their own power. Christ gives us the strength to fulfill the law. And the fullness of the law is love (Romans 13:10). Whoever rejoices in the law of the Ten Commandments sings the new song, because love is the

[125] Io. Eu. Tr. 65,1

[126] En. Ps. 39,4.

[127] En. Ps. 149,1.

[128] En. Ps. 66,6.

[129] En. 2 Ps. 32, s. 1,8.

fulfillment of the law.[130] The new song is thus nothing other than the new – and yet so old – love.[131]

"If all the earth is singing a new song, the whole earth is being built up even as it sings, for to sing is to build, provided, that is, that its song is not the old one. The desires of the flesh sing an old song, but the love of God sings a song that is new... Your love is itself a voice that sings to God; your love itself is the new song. Do you want proof of this? The Lord tells us: A new commandment I give you: that you love one another (Jo. 13:34). It is the whole earth that sings the new song, for that is where the house is under construction. The entire world is God's house..., love binds human beings together into one.[132] Because the new song consists of love, it is clear that it must be sung with life itself.[133]

Augustine will therefore also stress that the new song is the song of peace. Only those who preserve peace amongst one another sing the new song. Love praises God; discord among human beings is blasphemy.[134]

130 S. 33,1,1-2,2. En. Ps. 143,16.
131 S. 336,1.
132 En. Ps. 95,2.
133 En. 2 Ps. 32, s. 1,8.
134 En. Ps. 97,1. En. Ps. 149,2.

VI. Thanks and Supplication

1. The Prayer of Thanks

If we address thanksgiving and supplication in one and the same chapter, we are doing this because Augustine himself links the two. He says: "Thanking is one activity; the prayer of supplication is another. We offer thanks for something that is. We offer supplication so that something that does not yet exist might come to be".[1] There is thus a clear distinction between thanking and supplication. And yet, in both activities, God's goodness and magnanimity are central. We appeal to God's goodness to obtain something, but we offer thanks for gifts, for things we have obtained from God. That is also the case among human beings: we always thank someone else, never ourselves. That is why thanking is always associated with joy and happiness for what we have received.

Thanking is a form of praise because thanking means recognizing goodness in a particular manner and openly proclaiming it. In reference to God, this is the recognition of the Giver's goodness, and of the goodness of his gifts. What better frame of mind can we show than by saying: Thank God.[2] There is nothing shorter that can express it; there is nothing that is heard with greater joy; nothing more lofty to understand; nothing more fruitful to offer than: Thank God. Praise and thanksgiving go together: "What is a more holy offering of praise than an offering in thanksgiving? And for what must we offer God greater thanks than for his grace through Jesus Christ our Lord? The faithful know all this in the offering of the Church".[3] The last words are a definite allusion to the Eucharist. They also lead one to think of the text from

[1] En. 1 Ps. 103,3.
[2] Ep. 41,1.
[3] C. adv. Leg. 1,18,37.

Romans 8:32: Since God did not spare his own Son, but gave him up to benefit us all, we may be certain, after such a gift, that he will not refuse anything he can give. Where the bishop of Hippo cites this text in the past tense: "God has given us all with his Son", he refers to the divine Word as maker of the world. With him God has given us the whole world.[4] Where the bishop cites this text in the future: "God will, with himself, give us everything", he refers to the eternal kingdom of joy.[5]

The Latin word *gratia* has many meanings. It can mean: charm, favor, gift, love, grace, and also thanks. In many languages, we do not immediately see a connexion between grace and thanks. In Latin, there is one, and for that reason, Augustine can readily allude to *gratia* in the double meaning of grace and thanks, and switch from one meaning to the other. "Sisters and brothers, if you wish to express thanks (*gratias*), then drink grace in (*gratiam*). What does "drink in grace" mean? Learn to know grace, understand what grace is".[6] Our thanks to God consists merely of words. We cannot return the reality of the gift of grace because what is given to us has become a part of us, and it remains our possession. We cannot give God any grace:

> "Thanks be to his mercy, thanks be to his grace. He has saved us gratis. We say thanks, but we cannot give grace. We cannot return grace, we cannot repay it. There is nothing equal to it that we can give. We say thanks with words, but the reality of grace remains in us".[7]

Thus, if something is given to us, that which is given has become our possession. Let us just think of the many gifts people give one another. Other people give us presents so that we might enjoy them or use them. But that does not at all mean that nothing is required of us. The giver assumes that we value his gift, that we esteem it, and are grateful for it. Or, stated in other terms: the

[4] S. 334,2.
[5] Civ. 22,24,5.
[6] En. Ps. 144,10.
[7] En. 2 Ps. 88,14.

giver him- or herself wishes to be loved in his or her gift. "The divine gifts come from God, but they become our own on the condition that we love what we receive and express our thanks for it".[8] We must know who the giver is, otherwise it is impossible for us to thank him or her. Especially, we must not forget to express our thanks, and for that reason, we must remember the giver. If this does not occur, we shall be considered ungrateful people, and rightly so.

"If you do not know the person who you get a gift from, you cannot give thanks...What does it mean: to have received something in the full sense of the word "receive"? Knowing where you have it from...We, however, have not received the spirit of this world, but the Spirit who is from God. And as though Paul were asked: how do you tell the difference?, he went on to add: That we may know what things have been bestowed on us by God (1 Cor. 2:12)".[9]

In conjunction with this text, Augustine adds the following thought. Those who live according to the spirit of this world are the haughty, who are ungrateful toward God. Indeed, many possess God's gifts, but they do not honor him from whom they have received the gifts. One person might have greater intelligence, or a better memory than another, but the humble person who thanks God for little gifts is better than the haughty one who ascribes great gifts to himself. Humility is thus a precondition for thanks. The topic of the giver leads Augustine to play with the opposition: the gifts are of yourself, but they do not originate from you. Speaking of good will, faith, sanctity, righteousness, and consecrated virginity, then he says:

> "These are gifts of God, and they are yours also, but they are not of yourselves... Do not be surprised: it is both yours and not of you, for when we speak of our daily bread, we add immediately 'give us', lest it be thought to be of us".[10]

[8] S. 166,3,3.
[9] S. 283,2,2-3,3. Ep. 27,4.
[10] Ep. 188,2,6-7.

Speaking of gratitude entails naming those things concerning which one must be grateful. Those things for which we must be grateful to God go from the whole of Creation as God's gift to us to the internal gifts of grace through which God has wrought our salvation. The following text presents a nice summary of the reasons to be grateful to God:

> "You have made all things, they are yours. Thanks be to you. But you have made us over all of them. Thanks be to you. For we are your image and likeness. Thanks be to you. We have sinned, we have been sought. Thanks be to you. We have been negligent, we have not been neglected. Thanks be to you. When we despised you, we were not despised. In case we should have been forgotten your divinity and should lose you, you even took upon yourself our humanity. Thanks be to you. When and where can there not be thanks?"[11]

Augustine will stress, particularly against the Pelagians, who are firm believers in our own achievement, that we never offer thanks for that which simply lies within our own power. We needn't offer thanks for things we do ourselves. No one thanks him- or herself, but always another. For that reason, it would be ridiculous to thank God for things that we did ourselves, for things that he did not give or do.[12] The fault of the Pharisee was not that he gave thanks to God for his gifts (Luke 18:9-14), but that he thought that nothing had to be added to his righteousness. He was full of his own perfection, whereas the striving for perfection is a never-ending process. Smugly, he did not ask for more righteousness.[13] There is an obligation to be grateful to God. For what is worse for a human being, who is created in God's image and who knows God, than to be ungrateful? Praising God and being thankful are acts of respect for God; they are part of every religious service. For that reason, there is a relationship between honoring *(honorare)* or glorifying *(glorificare)* and thanking. To thank God is to honor

[11] S. Denis 20,6.

[12] Persev. 2,3.

[13] Pecc. mer. 2,5,6.

God. Augustine comments repeatedly on the text of Romans 1:20-21 in this sense: "From the creation of the world onward, his invisible nature, namely his eternal power and Godhead, becomes visible for the mind. Therefore, such people are not to be excused, for though they knew God, they did not render unto God the thanks that were his due".[14]

2. The Prayer of Petition

For most people, praying, in the first instance, has the significance of requests that are directed toward God. The prayer of praise has a much smaller place in their lives. Augustine is well aware of that fact. His faithful easily limit prayer to asking for something. Praying to God when only in need actually bears witness to an imperfect faith. Without directly censuring this, the Bishop of Hippo tries to teach his faithful what they must ask. He tries to educate them by always impressing upon their hearts that they must rise from asking for the most mundane things to asking for God himself. Even though God knows everything, we must direct prayers of petition to him for three reasons: 1) Because, as reasonable creatures, we should be subservient to God and therefore, we should relate temporal goods to eternal life. 2) We do this by asking for things that must fall to our own lot. 3) We also do this by asking for advice concerning what we must do.[15]

Asking for Worldly Goods

God does not forbid us to love what has been created, but he does forbid us to love it as if our ultimate happiness resided therein. God does not forbid eating, drinking, or having sexual relations.[16] God takes material human needs to heart. Following the example

[14] S. 68,4,5. S. Mai 126,6. Trin. 6,10,12. Spir. et litt. 13,22.
[15] Ep. 140,29,69.
[16] Ep. Io. Tr. 2,11-12.

of psalm 36:7 "You shall grant prosperity to human beings and animals, Lord, so great is your mercy, God," Augustine reminds his faithful not to be ashamed to think of God in this way. "The one who gives you sustenance, also sustains your horse and your sheep; and, to come to even smaller animals, he also sustains your fowl... you, God, have given life, you also give prosperity and health".[17] God cannot give his law to animals, but he can to human beings. Nevertheless, animals, too, fall under his care. Insofar as the inanimate things, living nature, and the animal world all around humanity is concerned, that which must be created, fed, controlled and regulated, they all come under God's care.[18] Augustine, here, is clearly referring to the needs of the small people among the population of North Africa. He also relates how he summoned those around him to pray, together with him, for relief from a toothache that was so bad that he could no longer speak.[19] What sick person does not ask for recovery? And what mother does not pray for her sick child, or what wife does not pray for her husband, and what husband does not pray for his wife? The faithful pray for all the sick.[20] The bishop knows that his countrymen frequently pray for rain.

"I am not saying: you should ask nothing from God. Ask as much as you can when you are in trouble. He has stopped the rain. You must ask him for rain... Sometimes, you see, God is mollified and grants what is asked for, and is only willing to grant it to those who ask for it".[21]

God's mercy is not only to be found in Heaven, but on earth as well. God's gifts are in part temporal and earthly, and in part eternal and heavenly. Earthly gifts are common to all human beings, both good and bad: sunshine and rain, light and air, the fruits and the various seasons, earthly comforts and sustenance, health,

[17] Io. Ev. Tr. 34,3.
[18] En. Ps. 145,14.
[19] Conf. 9,4,12.
[20] En. Ps. 59,7. S. Morin 16,2.
[21] S. Denis 21,9.

honor, the fellowship of friends, a happy family life, good children, and a good spouse. For that reason, many pray for fertility of a spouse and for progeny.[22] We can pray for honor and might, if it is for the purpose of helping others. We can pray for sufficient material wealth if it is for the sake of remaining healthy. We can pray for the soundness of body and soul. Because friendship gives joy, we can pray to have good friends. But the goal must always remain: living with God.[23] Bread, water, wine, meat, silver, or a beast of burden must be asked of God, and not of false gods, or demonic powers. All these goods comfort us in this care-filled existence. We are allowed to expect these of God and to ask him for them. They are all gifts from God. Because God created us with a soul and a body, he also cares for the soul and the body.[24] It is permitted to use present-day prosperity, which is also a source of happiness. We may use it as much as possible, to whatever extent is possible, when it is possible, so far as is possible. If this good fortune is present, then God should be thanked for the comfort. If this comfort is lacking, God must be thanked for his justice.[25]

But worldly goods are ambiguous, because sometimes they are to our advantage, and sometimes they are to our disadvantage. Poverty can be advantageous and wealth disadvantageous. Whoever squanders their money on frivolous ease and does nothing useful with it, do harm to themselves, and to others. An inconspicuous life can be advantageous, and a high position can be harmful. Sometimes, possessions and dignities are advantageous; advantageous for those who use this wealth, and disadvantageous for those who make poor use of it. Whoever permit themselves all sorts of refined pleasures readily forget God. We must be mindful of this fact, and ask God for worldly goods in moderation. Augustine presents examples from daily life. "If your child asks for a

22 En. Ps. 35,7. En. Ps. 66,2.
23 Ep. 130, 6,12-7,14.
24 En. Ps. 62,7.
25 En. Ps. 91,1.

knife or a sword, then you do not give it to the child, so as not to mourn his or her death. If your child whines all day long to sit on a horse, you do not set him or her on a horse, even if your child lies on the ground out of anger and throws a temper tantrum, because the horse could throw the little one and trample him or her to death."[26] It is useful to know what you are missing. But it is even better to know whom you must ask. God knows our needs and desires. But God wants us to ask to exercise our longing and to render our receptiveness greater. Therefore, we should not hesitate to ask. But, if we do not receive what we ask for, we must not be sad, for God knows what is good for us. Even the prayer of petition is a stimulus to direct us toward God and this stimulus applies to everyone, to Augustine himself as well as to his faithful. In the midst of the many evils in the world, there is no other hope.[27] We must pray that we do not succumb to evil.

"From whom you receive gratis the victory over concupiscence in order not to succumb to pleasure-seeking, from him also you receive the strength not to be broken by distress. Indeed, of God it is said: The Lord will give us what is agreeable (Ps. 85:13) and: From him comes my patience (Ps. 62:6)".[28]

3. The Unheard Prayer of Petition

According to Augustine, the fact that our questions regarding worldly goods often remain unheard is a daily experience. There is much suffering in this world. Out of love, we offer prayers of supplication for the life of a child or a loved one; we ask to be released from psychological suffering. And we are not heard, and we do not comprehend the "why" behind this suffering. In his letter on prayer, Augustine tries to track down something of the sense of pain and sadness. There he cites three reasons: 1) to

[26] S. 80,7. S. Denis 21,9.
[27] S. 80,1-2.
[28] En. 26,2 Ps. 118.

recover from our haughtiness; 2) to test our patience and love; 3) to atone for sins.[29] After the fall of Rome, with all its sorrow and misery, he says:

> "You are grieving over the collapse of timbers and stones, and the fact that those who were going to die any way have died. Lift up your heart, where your treasure is (Mt. 6:21). Your body is down below, and if your body feels dread, do not let it shake your heart... Nevertheless, you say: I did not want Rome to suffer such dreadful things. We can pardon you for not wanting it. Do not you be angry with God because he did want it. You are only human, he is God... But why does God want this? Why?... The Lord has his plans. These plans will become clearer, if the servant obeys... and from being a servant has become a friend according to the word of the Lord: I will call you no longer servants, but friends (John 15:15)".[30]

Augustine's response to suffering is that we cannot grasp the meaning of it, and, in faith, we must trust in God's insights. Even Augustine, praying for a sick friend at Carthage, once called out: "Lord, if you do not hear this prayer from your own, what do you hear?"[31] He knows the despair of human beings who call out: God does nothing about it! Why bother to pray? Why do bad people have overabundance and good people suffer hunger? The rich have never been needy and they have never known hunger. For that reason, a poor person says: "What have I done, poor wretch that I am, that I ask and do not receive?"[32] "Does God not mislead us with his promises? We serve God and receive what is bad. The things we value, the things we had received from him as something of value, he takes away from us, while malefactors, blasphemers, the haughty, and sowers of discontent have the wealth. Is God not a wrathful God?" Augustine replies that the wealth of the rich might well signify poverty. True wealth consists

[29] Ep. 130,14,25.
[30] S. Bibl. Cas. 1, 133,7.
[31] Civ. 22,8,3.
[32] S. Morin 16,2.

of spiritual goods.[33] Others ask: Why does God not make bread from stones (cf. Matthew 3:9)? They say: we belong to Christ, and now God has deserted us. Augustine answers: the fact that God does not hear us does not, by any means, signify that he has deserted us. God acts as a physician who applies a plaster or a bandage. He causes discomfort, but this is necessary in order for healing to occur. Repeatedly, Augustine comes back to the example of Paul who was not heard when he asked that the thorn in his flesh, which was caused by an angel of Satan's, be taken from him (2 Corinthians 12: 7-9). Elijah obtained bread from a raven (1 Kings 17:6), but we obtain the Word of God as bread.[34] Jesus' cry on the Cross: "My God, my God, why have you forsaken me?" (Matthew 27:46), and his prayer in the Garden of Olives: "My Father, if it be possible, let this cup pass from me" (Matthew 26:39), are other examples Augustine cites. It is as if God turned a deaf ear from the suppliant, but yet, he holds his compassion for the suppliant ready. In their trials, many call to God but are not heard; their prayer remains unheard for their benefit. God knows what he is doing. Trials are like a fire to refine gold.[35] That is especially true of the martyrs. They prayed: "Snatch my life from the fear for the enemy" (Psalm 64:2). They are not heard, but killed. And yet, God did not desert his servants, nor did he despise those who placed their hope in him, because "Whoever called the Lord and was abandoned? Whoever placed his hope in him and was left in the lurch by him?" (Sir. 2: 10). No, God was there, in the presence of his martyrs, and he gave them eternal life, while those who thought that the Christian faith was hollow and empty are devoured as corpses.[36] When God's saints were slaughtered, no one offered any resistance, no one defended them, or prevented it. It was as if God were no longer God and had deserted and forgotten them. But, just as he did not desert Christ on the Cross, he

[33] En. 2 Ps. 33,14-15 and 20. En. Ps. 72,6.
[34] En. 2 Ps. 90,6. Ep. Io. Tr. 6,7-8.
[35] En. 2 Ps. 21,3-5.
[36] En. Ps. 63,2.

did not desert his saints.[37] Even if we, correctly, ask God for something good and he does not grant it, we must not lose courage. Then, there is the danger that one could fall away from God and regard faith in him as worthless. Some say: if God gives no worldly goods, it is better to desert him and honor a god that does provide such goods.[38] For that reason, Augustine warns his fellow believers: "You say: how fervently, and how frequently have I asked God for something without being heard"! Augustine responds to that with the question: "If God does not grant it, does he then mean nothing more to you?"[39] And he has God say: "If I save you, then I am your God, but if I castigate, then I am no longer your God"![40] Within this context, Augustine refers repeatedly to the example of Job. He remained faithful to God, in prosperity and in adversity. He kept praising God, because God always remains our Father.[41]

We must therefore leave to God's wisdom what he wishes to give us, and when he wishes to give it. When through our prayers our own wishes are fulfilled, it does not mean that we have prayed in the right way.[42] Some people construe the prayer of supplication as a sort of legal relationship: "I give something to God, and I must get something back in return". "Indeed, I want to praise God, someone says, if he gives me something in exchange for this praise. For who praises a human being in an entirely disinterested fashion? Those who praise a human being expect a certain reward. Must, then, the person who praises God, expect, ask for, or hope for no reward?" God has, indeed, held out the prospect of such a reward to us, but that does not mean that he will grant us everything we desire. As our Father, he knows what is good for us.[43] God wants to give himself. But, out of love, he postpones our salvation, for good

[37] En. Ps. 43,2.
[38] S. Mai 15,2.
[39] En. Ps. 85,8. En. Ps. 144,19-22.
[40] En. Ps. 49,24.
[41] S. Mai 15,1-3. En. 2 Ps. 32, s. 1,2-3. En. 2 Ps. 33,3-4. En. 2 Ps. 48,9.
[42] S. 354,7,7.
[43] En. Ps. 146,1.

reason, and not out of helplessness. Not because he cannot help us at this moment, but to draw as large a number of human beings to him as possible. [44]

4. Praying for Spiritual Goods

Thus far, supplication for worldly goods was the issue, in which case, we are far from being heard all the time. At any rate, we do not always know where our advantage lies; we do not even know how we ought to pray (Romans 8:26). But we are always heard if we pray for eternal life, namely, if we pray for our own salvation.[45] In the interpretation of the text "Whatsoever you shall ask in my name, I will do" (John 14:13), Augustine emphasizes that the name Jesus means "savior". Everything we ask for that does not contribute to our being saved, to our salvation, we do not ask in the name of our Savior and Redeemer. This is not to say that he will immediately do what we ask, but we may be assured that sometime, he will do it. By way of example, Augustine cites the prayer that the Kingdom of God should come. Whoever abides in Christ can ask no more than that which is in agreement with Christ, that is to say, that which is in agreement with our salvation.[46] Thus, the prayer for our salvation is always heard.

Augustine regards the following as eternal goods: eternal life, the incorruptibility and immortality of the body and soul, the community with the angels, the heavenly city, inexhaustible worth, the Father, and the fatherland:[47]

> We should be longing for these benefits with infinite desire, pray for them with tireless perseverance, not with long speeches but with the evidence of our desire. Desire is praying always, even if the tongue is silent. If you desire always, you are praying always. When

[44] En. 2 Ps. 34,9.
[45] En. Ps. 59,7.
[46] Io. Ev. Tr. 73. 81,4. 102,2.
[47] S. 80,7.

> does prayer nod off to sleep? When desire grows cold. So let us beg for these everlasting benefits with insatiable eagerness, let us seek these good things which, after all, benefit those who have them, and cannot possibly do them harm.

"Love itself implores. Love itself prays. Against it God who gave it, cannot close his ears. Be free of anxiety; let love ask, and God's ears are there. What you wish does not happen, but what is advantageous does happen. Therefore, whatever we shall ask, John says, we shall receive from him. I have already said that, if you understand the words 'for our salvation' there is no problem. If not 'for our salvation', there is a problem, and a big one".[48]

We must not ask God for things the non-believers ask for as well. We must ask him for something more, something great. Indeed, we must ask him for things that are necessary for this life, but God is our greatest treasure. The thirst for him is, at this time, our prayer of petition.[49] The prayer of petition is an exercise in longing for spiritual goods. This corresponds to the nature of prayer, because praying is a spiritual activity. Therefore, our prayer is more acceptable the more it achieves the realisation of its nature. The more our spirit is uplifted above fleshly lust, the greater the effect of a spiritual work.[50] Thus, the prayer of petition must signify a clarification and purification of our desires so that our thirst for God remains sound or is aroused. Postponement of an answer will increase our desire, as the wind that strikes the fire does, indeed, push the flame aside, only to have it flare up all the more intensely.[51]

For that reason, God found it necessary to mix the sweetness of life with the bitterness of testing and suffering.[52] Because if worldly goods were totally good, and not mixed with evil, they should readily be regarded as the highest that a human being can

48 Ep. Io. Tr. 6,8.
49 En. Ps. 62,14.
50 S. 210,6,9.
51 En. Ps. 87,14. En. Ps. 142,12.
52 S. Denis 21,9.

attain. In addition, we discover that worldly goods are given to good people and bad alike. If God were to give them only to good people, bad people would think that God had to be served in order to acquire worldly goods. Should God give them only to the bad, weaklings would recoil from converting, for then the good would miss the good things of life. The fact that God gives them to good people is a comfort for them on their pathway through life. The fact that God also gives them to bad people is an encouragement to the good people to long for higher goods. If God withholds his gifts from some, it should be remembered that he never withholds himself. If a bad person looses all his worldly goods, he has nothing more. It makes no sense for him to turn back within himself, because within his innermost recesses he has nothing. The good person, by contrast, knows that God is present within him. Job's wealth was an inner wealth, for his heart was full of God.[53] Augustine clarifies these thoughts with the example of an ant. In the summer, an ant stores a supply in its nest, in order to have food for the winter. Thus, in times of surfeit, Christians must store up spiritual food in their hearts so that they can fetch it out in times of trial.[54] In another sermon, Augustine expresses the same thought in an entirely concrete manner:

> "You say: bad things are done in the world, harsh, vile, hateful things. It is a foul world. It should not be loved. Yes, that it is what it is like, and even so it is loved. The house is in ruins, and we are too lazy to move. When mothers or wet-nurses see their babies growing bigger, and it is no longer right for them to go on to being fed on milk, and yet they are still tiresomely demanding the breast, mothers or wet-nurses smear their nipples with something bitter, to stop them seeking forever. This puts the infant off, so that it would not demand milk any more. God has filled the world with all sorts of bitterness. And here are you, panting for it, here are you, clinging to it, here are you, sucking it. Only from this and that in the

[53] En. Ps. 120,8.
[54] En. Ps. 66,3. En. Ps. 43,2.

> world do you get any pleasure. How long for? Suppose the world was all sweetness, think how it would be loved. Do these things offend you? Choose another life. Love God".[55]

We are turned away from the world by a little bitterness with the aim of reaching toward a higher world and toward God. Even by means of trials, God wants to draw us toward himself. As examples of such trials, Augustine reports: people have suffered an injury, they mourn the death of a dear one, they suffer under the loneliness of banishment, far away from their homeland, their vineyard is laid waste by hail, they grieve for a friend who has been unfaithful.[56] Perhaps we sometimes think we are not weak and we require no purification. But this is not Augustine's assessment. If a human being does not see his or her own weakness, that is, indeed, most dangerous, for then that person does not know that he or she is mortal and limited.

The prayer of supplication must thus be directed especially toward spiritual goods. Spiritual goods, however, exhibit a great variety. We must pray in order to be liberated from our vices.[57] We offer supplication to possess, to an ever greater degree, the gift of love of God and our neighbors.[58] There are many ways of praying for ourselves. If God is our life, we may expect from him the gifts of wisdom, piety, righteousness, and love, which we do not, automatically, have from ourselves. We must ask to be good people, for what is more unfortunate than possessing a good country house, good clothing, a good flock of sheep, good sandals, without being good oneself? All those things are good, but they do not suffice to make a person good. Thus, ask God to be made good yourself because the good spirit of God gives a good will to human beings (cf. Luke 11:13).[59] Our prayer, however, is not directed solely at ourselves. We should pray for all people. In a

[55] S. 311,17,14.
[56] En. Ps. 49,22.
[57] S. 80,3.
[58] En. 17,2 Ps. 118.
[59] Io. Ev. Tr. 19,12. S. Lambot 1.

sermon, Augustine tells how someone asked the martyr Fructuosus to pray for him. But Fructuosus answered: “I ought to pray for the catholic Church, spread from East to West”. In recounting the story, Augustine comments: whoever prays for the whole also prays for each one individually, without passing anyone over.[60] Whoever prays for the whole Body of Christ passes no one by. The prayer of petition for a brother in the faith is more pleasing to God if it is coupled with an offering of love. When we pray for one another, our prayers for each other flow together in love. Thus, Jesus prayed for all those who believed in him, or would, in future, believe in him: “Not for their sakes alone do I pray, but also for them who, by their word, will believe in me” (John 17:20). Jesus did not pray for the righteous of the first Covenant, because they had already died, and, because of their great merits, they were at rest in God.[61]

What is more splendid than praying for the whole human race, for the entire world, for all peoples, that they might adhere to God? Every believer prays for those who stand outside the Church, just as the faithful of Jerusalem prayed for the non-believer Saul. We should pray that our friends or our spouse might arrive at faith.[62] Merely proclaiming the faith is not enough. It must be coupled with praying for all those in error, for all non-believers and all catechumens. Faith comes from God, as a gift. For that reason, we thank God whenever others come to believe. We ourselves cannot bring that about.[63] Never was there a time that the Church had no prayers for the non-believers and its foes. She did not only pray that God should give faith to the non-believers, but also for perseverance of all the believers in the faith.[64] Every believer must pray for the dead. As a mother, in her liturgy, the Church knows prayers of petition for all the dead,

60 S. 273,2,2.
61 Ep. 20,2. S. Denis 13,10. Io. Ev. Tr. 109,2.
62 En. 1 Ps. 103,3. S. 110,1. S. 168,6,6.
63 Ep. 217,1,1-2,7.
64 Persev. 23,63.

including those who no longer have anyone to pray for them. It is to the benefit of the dead who merited that when they were still alive. But, because we do not know who they are, we should pray for all the dead.[65] We pray, however, not only that people might arrive at faith, but also for all who are in need, and especially, for all prisoners and all the sick.[66]

From the many references to Matthew 5:44 "But I tell you: Love your enemies and pray for those who persecute you", we can see what an impression the text made upon Augustine.[67] Jesus' prayer on the Cross for his enemies "Father, forgive them, for they do not know what they are doing" (Luke 23:34), and of Stephen "Lord, do not post this sin to their account" (Acts 7:60), are Augustine's great examples.[68] Praying for your enemies is certainly not easy. Many pray against their enemies instead of for them; Augustine calls this "praying in an incompetent way". The Church prayed for Saul, not against him. In this way, he was transformed from a Saul into a Paul.[69] By praying against an enemy, one always harms oneself, and one even loses one's share in Heaven. Praying for the ruination or the death of an enemy is a bad prayer. That is praying with hatred and not with love, so that wicked people might improve their lot.[70] If we hate others, and thus, our enemies, then we, ourselves, are bad. The result is not that there is one fewer bad person, but rather, that there is one more bad person, namely the person who hates the evildoer.[71] Indeed, we may hate evil and someone else's faults, but we must love the person. As a human being, the other person is a creature of God, but, as a sinner, he is a creature of his own making.[72]

[65] Cura mort. 4,6 and 18,22.
[66] Ep. 111,7.
[67] S. 49,7,7-10,11.
[68] S. 149,15-16. En. Ps. 7,5. En. Ps. 69,3.
[69] S. 56,3,3.
[70] En. Ps. 139,7. En. Ps. 37,14. En. Ps. 39,4. En. Ps. 54,6-7.
[71] En. 2 Ps. 30, s. 3,2.
[72] En. Ps. 138,28.

"You look upon your enemy, opposing you, raging, biting with words, irritating with insults, pursuing with hatred. You, observe there that he is a human person. You see all these hostile things that have been done by a human person, and you see in him what he was made by God. That he was made a human being, he was made by God. But that this human person hates you, she or he made it. That this person envies you, he or she made. You should say in your mind: Lord, be propitious to him or her. Forgive him or her their sins. Strike fear in them, change them. You do not love in them what they are but what you wish them to be. Thus when you love an enemy, you love a brother or sister. Therefore, perfect love is the love of an enemy".[73]

It is always possible that someone who lives badly might convert and that a foe might turn into a friend and fellow believer. For this reason, despairing in a human being is not good. Tomorrow, he may be our brother. We do not even know ourselves; how, then, should we be in a position to know another person to the core and pass an absolute judgment over him or her? Someone who is unfavorably predisposed toward us may be better than we.[74] But sometimes, we fail completely with many words and warnings to bring others to a better disposition. Then, all we can do is pray for them. Some sinners even bring us to despair. Augustine gives us the following advice: consider "to whom" you are supplicating and do not heed "for whom" you supplicate.[75] God knows whom he has called and pre-destined for eternal salvation, but we human beings do not know that. For that reason, the calling, or predestination by God, may never be an impediment to praying for all people, without exception. We pray that all might be saved and that the number of the holy may come to fullness. If we do this, we cooperate with God. It is readily possible that they are predestined for the grace of selection precisely because of, and through the agency of our prayers.[76]

[73] Ep. Io. Tr. 8,10.

[74] En. Ps. 39,4. En. Ps. 55,20. En. Ps. 139,2.

[75] En. Ps. 54,8. En. Ps. 55,12.

[76] Persev. 22,60. En. Ps. 147,7.

5. Asking God Himself

Finally, we come to the climax of every prayer of petition. The purest form of prayer of petition consists of asking God himself. Those who ask God are always heard. If nothing needs to be asked apart from God, just ask God for himself, and he will hear you. As you are still speaking, he will say: "See, I am with you" (Isaiah 65:24). All that I have given you is worth less than I.[77] In life, many temporary choices are possible: some choose the army, a career as an attorney, a job in science, others want to devote themselves to commerce or agriculture. Careers are chosen because of the wages attached to them. But one must not expect any wages from God; he wants to be loved in a disinterested fashion, and even to be our highest reward. If you love God for any reason other than himself, then, in point of fact, you regard that other thing as being of greater value than God.[78] There are people who raise the question: "What should I pray for? What shall I ask?", to which Augustine always replies: appeal to God as God, love God as God. "Hardly anyone prays to the Lord for his own sake. It is quite easy to demand all sorts of things from the Lord, and not to ask for the Lord himself, as if that which he gives could be more pleasing than the giver himself".[79] Ask for the entire earth, the whole sea, all the islands, ask for the air and the heavens, there is nothing better to be found than he who made everything. All things are dear to us because they are all attractive. But they are not more attractive than he. God wants to give himself and if you ask for something less, you insult him and do damage to yourself:[80]

> "It is with the heart one asks, with the heart one seeks, with the heart one knocks, to the heart the door is opened. But the heart that asks for this in the right way, knocks and seeks in the right way,

[77] En. 2 Ps. 33,9. En. Ps. 85,8.
[78] En. Ps. 72,32. En. Ps. 134,11.
[79] En. Ps. 76,2.
[80] En. 1 Ps. 34,12.

> must be a pious heart, first and foremost loving God freely and for nothing (that, after all, is what piety is), and not setting some reward which one expects from him, in addition to himself".[81]

Many, in fact, do not invoke God as they should. They expect something else of him, but they do not seek him, himself. They ask for health, a rich wife, good children and a good family life. I ask you, so Augustine says, ask for him, himself, as well. For all these things are not more pleasing than he, himself, nor are they comparable to him. Only he truly invokes God who prefers God, himself, above all things.[82] But the vision of God and his promises are not yet reality; their fulfillment lies in the future. Our God is our hope, and for that reason, we ask for God himself. For a long time, we long for him, whom we would possess for all time. Now our longing is still an exercise in receiving God, who wants to give himself.[83] Bad people expect only things of the present; good people expect things of the future. The former are satisfied with transitory things; the latter have a hope that is certain. Many esteem consumer goods; few esteem inner resources. But Augustine knows the human heart sufficiently well to know that there are many who doubt or despair with respect to a life to come. They say: "Who knows if it is true!".[84]
Seeking God for God's own sake can be translated in terms of Jesus:

> "How many seek Jesus only that he may do them good temporally. One person has a business transaction; he seeks the intervention of the clergy. Another is hardpressed by one more powerful; he flees to the church. Another wishes an intervention on his behalf with a person with whom he has little influence. So one, so another. Today the church is filled with such people. Jesus is scarcely sought for Jesus' sake… Seek me for my sake".[85]

[81] S. 91,3,3.
[82] En. Ps. 144,22.
[83] En. Ps. 39,7. En. Ps. 83,3.
[84] En. Ps. 52,8. En. Ps. 4,8-9.
[85] Io. Ev. Tr. 25,10.

With respect to disinterested love directed toward God or Jesus, Augustine readily uses the example of love within a marriage. Whoever loves a woman for the sake of her dowry does not really love her. And conversely: a woman who loves her husband because he has given her something, or even a great deal, does not love him in a pure manner. Just as people should love each other freely in order to be able to speak of true love, how, then, should we love God other than freely? A wife who loves her spouse in a disinterested way is not interested in obtaining all sorts of things from him, things that will make her happy, but rather, she keeps him, through whom she is rendered happy, before her eyes.[86] The example of the betrothed couple is known as well. A young man has made his girlfriend quite a pretty ring, but she seems to think more highly of the ring than she does of her young fiançé.

"Certainly she loves what her fiançé gave. Yet if she should say: This ring is enough for me, I no longer wish to see his face – what sort of woman would she be?...You love the gold instead of the human person, you love the ring instead of the fiançé. But if you love the ring instead of your fiançé... this gift is not a pledge that unites the two more intimately, but has become a source of aversion. A fiançé gives a pledge token for this, of course, that in his token he himself should be loved. So God gave you the entire world. Love him who made it for you".[87]

In prayer, fear of the Lord also plays a role. Augustine distinguishes between two sorts of fear. There is the fear of the slave who carries out an order out of fear of punishment, but without love. In prayer, there is no room for slavish fear of God, because such fear signifies no real love of God, for love presupposes freedom. A love that is not a free gift is an internal contradiction. Love cannot be forced. But, in addition to slavish fear, there is also a good fear, namely the fear of losing God, and the fear that one might not remain in his love. Indeed, there is room for this fear in prayer.[88]

86 En. Ps. 55,17. En. 1 Ps. 34,12.

87 Ep. Io. Tr. 2,11.

88 En. 2 Ps. 18,10. S. 17,1. En. 22,6 Ps. 118.

Nevertheless, even slavish fear can grant access to love to the extent that it can effect a beginning of conversion. The fear of God makes wounds, as does a doctor's instrument. But do not be anxious, love will heal the wounds of fear.[89]

6. The Our Father as a Rule for Prayer

The Disciples heard Jesus praying, and through them, we hear Jesus praying as well. Several of his prayers have been recorded. He taught us how we ought to pray. Augustine extends Jesus' prayers by putting some words from the psalms in his mouth, such as, for example: "God, have pity on me, have pity on me, for in you does my soul place its trust" (Psalm 57:2). Of course, he also refers to texts from the New Testament, especially to the priestly prayer in John, such as: "Then he turned his eyes heavenward and said: Father, the hour has come. Glorify your son, that your son might glorify you" (John 17:1).[90] Jesus revealed his prayers to us in this way so that we could learn not only of his conversations, but also of his prayers to the Father. Of course, this applies in the highest degree to the Our Father (Matthew 6:9-13). In that prayer, he impressed upon our hearts all the rules of a holy longing. The Our Father is a mirror in which we can see the life of the righteous who live from faith, even though we are not without sin, and even though we are not perfectly righteous. The words that Jesus taught us in the Our Father are the form of our desires. We are not free to ask for something other than what stands there.[91] We are the ones who need the words of the Our Father to make us aware of what we are asking, not to instruct God, or to appease. We now wish to see how Augustine interprets the different prayers of the Our Father.

Our Father who art in Heaven - this is an act of praise of him to whom we direct our prayer. At the same time, it is a request for

[89] Ep. Io. Tr. 9,4-8.
[90] En. Ps. 56,5. Io. Ev. Tr. 104,2.
[91] Perf. iust. 8,18-19. S. 56,3,4.

God's favorable disposition toward us. It is a grace that we have God as Father, and that he is willing to accept us as his children. If God acknowledges himself as Father, we may place our childlike trust in him, because it is normal for the relationship between a father and his children to be an affectionate one. Everyone, even the poor and insignificant, may call God Father. Calling God Father also alters our relations to other people. Because we all have a common Father, we are all each other's brothers and sisters: the master and the slave, the emperor and the soldier, the rich and the poor, the distinguished ones of noble origin and the unattractive of low degree. "In heaven" is not an indication of place, but means that God dwells in the holy and the righteous. We are God's temple (1 Corinthians 3:17), and by being righteous, we invite God to dwell in us.

Hallowed be thy name – This name is always holy, but we pray not only that we, but that all people, may keep that name holy, and that the mention of his name may always occur with respect and fear of giving offense. The fact that God's name is not disdained benefits not God, but us. Nevertheless, the holiness of human beings is the glory of God. By praying for this, therefore, we wish ourselves well. We ask that God might make us holy.

Thy kingdom come – God rules for all time, thus now as well. Whether we like it or not, his kingdom is coming. But we ask that his kingdom might come for us, and that it might be made manifest to all people. Here, too, we are also praying for ourselves, namely, that we might belong to his kingdom, in this life, merely provisionally, but later in full reality. If we speak now of the kingdom of God, we must not forget that it is still being convened and built up here on earth. God's dominion is not yet complete, and the power of his kingdom is not yet fully developed. For us, this means that we pray to be found worthy to rule with God in his realm, for the time being in an incipient way, but after this life, in a much deeper way.[92]

[92] Io. Ev. Tr. 68,2.

Thy will be done on earth as it is in heaven – Here we pray that God's commandments might be obeyed by us, not slavishly, but in free and loving obedience, in this way working toward God's intended aim with this world, as the angels do in heaven. In addition, we ask that all people might convert and serve God obediently. By doing God's will, all the patriarchs, prophets, apostles, and those who lived according to the Spirit, are holy. They are, so to speak, heaven; by comparison with them, we are the earth. Heaven and earth can also refer to the spirit and the body of a human being. It means that the entire human being, with spirit and body, performs God's commandments. Heaven and earth can also mean Jesus Christ and the church; as your will was done in Jesus, so must it be done in the church as well. In the church, too, those who live according to the Spirit are heaven, and those who live according to the flesh are the earth. Thus, the church may be regarded as heaven, and the church's non-believing enemies, as the earth. Here Augustine discusses at great length praying for the enemy. Finally, heaven and earth can also be symbols for man and woman; both heaven and earth, both man and woman, should do God's will. In this process, we should bear in mind that if God's will is done by us, God brings this to pass in us.

Give us this day our daily bread – With these words, we pray for everything we need to live here on earth, because bread is a summary of all that is necessary to sustain life. The fact that all people (even the wealthiest of all) pray for bread is an indication that everyone stands as a beggar before God, for no one can call him- or herself the creator of bread; it is a gift from God. Here, too, we pray for bread, not only for ourselves, but for bread for all people. Bread can also mean the sacrament of the Body of Christ, which we receive daily. Bread can also stand for spiritual food, which we need every day. Because the Eucharist is not celebrated every day everywhere, Augustine prefers the latter interpretation: the daily consideration and the daily implementation of the Divine commandments, that is to say, feeding ourselves daily with God's Word, with readings from the Scriptures, and hymns. Everyone needs the Word of God.

And forgive us our trespasses, as we forgive those who have trespassed against us – This, of course, refers first of all to all our own sins, for which we ask forgiveness of God. Even though we have been baptized, we remain guilty, for we can never keep ourselves entirely free of sin, especially of venial sin. And yet, we must not neglect these venial sins but rather, we must ask for forgiveness for them. It is not enough to do this with our lips alone. Our hearts must be involved in doing so in all forthrightness. Otherwise, the desire to improve is lacking. If this desire is lacking, then this important prayer becomes a lie. And whoever lies cannot possibly obtain what he or she requests. Such a person cannot expect any result to come from his or her prayer. In the case of Matthew, the prayer for the forgiveness of sins appears to be the most important, because by praying in this way we enter into an agreement with God: God will grant us forgiveness, if we forgive others for their sins. Precisely because there was no sacrament for the daily forgiveness of sins in Augustine's day, the Our Father had the sacramental power to forgive venial sins. In that sense, he can say: "The Our Father is, as it were, our daily baptism".[93] But Augustine is not merely thinking of spiritual guilt here, but also of material debt, under which the poor are often subjected to severe suffering. Discharging the monetary debt of a poor person is a Christian act. Making a profit with someone else's money is reprehensible.

Augustine devotes even more thought to granting forgiveness to one's enemies. Without loving one's enemy, it is impossible to grant forgiveness. He stresses that it is not impossible to pray for one's enemy. Some raise the objection: Christ was able to do that, but we weak human beings cannot do it. To refute them, Augustine refers to the example of Stephen, even though he does admit that few are able to love their enemies. We need God's help to do that. We must therefore pray that we will be in a position to do that. The most important thing is not to utter this prayer, but to apply it in practice, to be a performer of it. No one is our enemy

[93] S. 213,8,8.

by virtue of his or her human nature, which is common to us all, and by virtue of which we are brothers and sisters to one another. In addition, granting forgiveness to another person is to grant him or her the possibility of self-improvement. Certainly, in the case of Christians, it would be impossible to speak of taking revenge. Care must be taken that anger does not expand to hatred. Hatred is deeply-rooted anger. Hating someone else is tantamount to killing him or her.

And lead us not into temptation – God never leads us into temptation, but he allows it so that we learn to know ourselves. Leading into temptation is not the same thing as being tempted. Being tempted is something unavoidable, because without being tempted, no one can acquire virtue. We also ask for God's help not to fall into agreement with the temptation or to succumb to it. Augustine will take the position against the Pelagians that we cannot, by dint of our own power, withstand all temptations, but that we require Divine grace to do so. We therefore pray that we have the courage to fight against our evil desires, and that God will not abandon us in the fight. In that sense, we must "with a true and steadfast frame of mind, imbued with the Spirit, watch with Christ, and appeal to him with the prayer that he taught us, so that, with his help, we are in a position to do what he has commanded".[94]

But deliver us from evil – This prayer is, in a certain sense, included in the previous one. Firstly, we ask to be saved from the evil we have committed. But this prayer is also oriented toward the future, for we do not live in everlasting bliss where we shall not have to endure evil, but we hope and pray to be spared from all evil in the future.

Of these seven prayers, the first three remain in eternity; the holiness, the kingdom, and the will of God are eternal goods. The four latter prayers pertain to this life.[95] There is a certain agreement among these seven prayers, the seven beatitudes, and the

[94] S. Wilmart 6,3.
[95] Ench. 115,30.

seven gifts of the Holy Spirit. The Our Father is truly the norm for our prayers. Whoever says anything that cannot be traced back to the Our Father, prays in a fleshly manner, even though it may not be in a manner that is not allowed. And yet, Augustine finds that praying in a fleshly manner is not allowed, because Christians should, in point of fact, pray in a spiritual manner. But quite a lot of what we ask for can fortunately be traced back to the prayers of the Our Father.[96]

[96] S. Dom. m. 2,4,15-11,39. Ep. 130,11,21-12,22. S. 56,4,5-14,19. S. 57,2,2-12,12. S. 58,2,2-10,12. S. 59,1,1-5,8. Persev. 2,4-5,9.

VII. Praying and Human Imperfection

If we had no difficulty in praying, then our praying would not be human. Augustine seems to have an acute insight into the difficulties. One has the impression that here he took the path of most mortals. He himself confesses: "I have often experienced, in myself, as well as in others, that the words we utter differ from the things we think... which frequently comes over me in the singing of a hymn".[1] Augustine asks contemplative monks, whose prayers are certainly more reflective, and more quiet than his own, to remember him in their prayers. He says that his prayers are often disturbed and attenuated by the darkness and frenzy of mundane activities and by so many material cares and worries of other people, that he scarcely finds the time to draw a breath. He hopes that God, with the aid of their prayers, will free him of every anxiety.[2] Nearly always, he returns to the topic of the difficulty of concentrating. A motley lot of imaginary images give us no rest and they also jolt our spirit away from its inwardness. Even in prayer, we can hardly achieve any peace because of the many deceitful images of which our spirit is full. Indeed, we want to return to what we were thinking of, but then, something else intervenes.[3] Augustine speaks of our spirit flitting over and back:

> "He whom we praise is very great, but our competence to praise him is still inadequate. Will the praise-singer ever match the excellence of the one who is praised? A person stands there praising God, perhaps for quite a long time. And often enough, while his lips are moving in song, his thoughts are flitting to and fro because of so many desires and concerns. Soul, what is the reason that you are so preoccupied by caring for earthly and perishable things? What has happened? Our reason was standing there, so to speak, intent on

[1] Mag. 13,42.
[2] Ep. 48,1.
[3] En. Ps. 136,7. En. Ps. 37,11.

> praising God, but our soul was vacillating, wavering hither and thither between various desires or worries about its own business...Why are you so preoccupied about other matters?...The soul replies to you: I am praising him as best I can, in my frail, puny, feeble way... Relieve me of this body that weighs down the soul, and then I will praise the Lord. Dismantle this earthly dwelling that clogs the mind as it considers many things, and then I will withdraw from the many and flow with all my being toward the one. Then I will praise the Lord".[4]

No one needs to flatter him- or herself; among the many prayers we say, it remains an exception when we remain with God in quiet pleasure. Indeed, we do want to stay firmly with God, but our hearts also flee, as it were, from themselves.

"Truly, my brothers and sisters, in my human condition and from my own human experience I will speak to yours: let each of us bring his own heart under scrutiny and examine him- or herself without flattery or pretence... Let each one closely observe what goes on in the human heart, and see how our many prayers are for the most part so hindered by idle thoughts that the heart can scarcely stand before its God. It wants to take hold of itself so that it may stand, but somehow runs away from itself, and can find no fence to shut itself in... so that it quietly may be delighted with its God. Scarcely one such prayer comes its way amid a great deal of praying".[5]

Augustine then notes that we must not think that we are the only ones to experience this, that it does not come over others. He refers to David's exclamation: "I found my heart to pray to you" (2 Samuel 7:27), as if his heart were accustomed to fleeing from him, and he continually had to run after it. And yet, the fleeing of our hearts must not be an excuse for not praying. Calling to God with one's whole heart is an outstanding prayer, but, in the case of most people, it is a rarity.[6] It is as if we forgot before whom we are

[4] En. Ps. 145,6.

[5] En. Ps. 85,7.

[6] En. 29,1 Ps. 118.

standing, and before whom we prostrate.[7] The Christian life here on earth is never perfect. It is a never-ending upward progress. We can benefit from prayer in order to cause a small spark of love to flare up higher.[8] And yet, however perfect a Christian might be, he does not have his thoughts and desires within his power. They constitute a portion of his weakened nature. For that reason, Augustine asks: "What do you do with your thoughts? What do you do with the unrest and the mass of stirred-up desires? You give them no chance to become a reality... And yet, they sometimes divert your attention, and carry you away; this occurs especially in the case of prayer... I see where the body lies, but ask me whither the mind flies... The mind is dragged along, as it were, by a tidal wave, and cast up here and there by a storm".[9] Thus, Augustine does not hesitate to compare the rising up and ebbing of our thoughts in prayer with a stormy sea.

Concentration in prayer is, indeed, difficult. Distractions criss-cross our prayers. Looked at from the human perspective, they would be insults. Here, Augustine alludes to what happens in a conversation between two people. "If someone is engaged in a conversation with me and suddenly addresses a servant, I experience that as an insult. What friend would tolerate someone who would begin a conversation with him or her, then turn to chat with someone else? Who would tolerate you if you pestered a judge for clarification or advice, and you received him in a certain place so that he could hear you, but, once the conversation has begun, you run away from him to talk to a friend?"[10] That would be intolerable for human beings. Fortunately, God is much more tolerant.

When praying, other obstacles present themselves, obstacles over which we have more control than distractions. We can also lose the desire to pray, and become negligent. Then, all the ardor has disappeared from our prayer. Neglect stands opposite perse-

[7] S. 56,9,12.
[8] S. 178,10,11.
[9] En. Ps. 140,18.
[10] En. Ps. 85,7. En. Ps. 140,18.

verance. We must ask God for perseverance in prayer, because it is a gift from him.

"As long as we are in this world we must entreat God not to take away from us either our prayer or his mercy; that is, we must ask that we may perseveringly pray and he may perseveringly have mercy on us. Many people grow weary of prayer. In their first fervor after conversion they pray ardently, then later more lazily, then rather coldly, and at last quite negligently. They think themselves secure... But the Lord commanded in the gospel that we must pray always, and not give up (Lk. 18:1)".[11]

Augustine speaks broadly about the distaste we experience if we must frequently repeat things. In the case of religious instruction, distaste of this kind can easily occur.[12] But, this is no rarity in the case of praying, either. For this phenomenon, Augustine uses the words "distaste, boredom" *(taedium)* or "aversion" *(fastidium)*. In modern translation, we should also be able to speak of "dryness". For our part, we must try to avoid and to overcome aversion from praying as much as possible, but that is not to say that it cannot come over us as a trial from God. Since Augustine describes the four great temptations in our ascent to God: the temptation of error, the difficulty in doing good, distaste and boredom with God's word and the temptation of power, then the third temptation is particularly important for our subject.

"I am speaking now to those who have passed through the first two temptations, which, I admit, are familiar to many people... Some are then entrapped by the third temptation, the trial of boredom with the tedium of this life, so that he or she may sometimes find no pleasure at all in reading or prayer... How can this happen? It can only be the effect of tiredness of the soul... You are glad to have escaped the dangers of ignorance and concupiscence. But watch out, for weariness and boredom may kill you. This too is no light temptation. Recognize yourself in it, and cry out to the Lord to deliver you from your plight in this matter as well".[13]

[11] En. Ps. 65,24.

[12] Cat. rud. 10,14-14,22.

[13] En. Ps. 106,6 and 11.

Praying without distaste, without depression, without anxiety, and without aversion is a gift from God. Thus, even this dryness has its meaning and sense, for it can prevent us from becoming proud, and it will compel us to acknowledge humbly that even joy in the spiritual life is God's gift. Augustine knew this joy himself, and he refers to it frequently. The joy renders something that is bothersome much easier. What we do eagerly is not so difficult. It is good to pray that we might be capable of living up to God's commandments, for our will must do something. With faithful and persistent prayers, and with works of compassion, we must continually ask for the gift of "ease", even with regard to the act of praying.[14] But Augustine is sufficiently realistic to recommend that devotion in praying not be forced, and turned into distaste. When devotion cannot persist, it makes no sense to try to hold fast to it by force. But devotion must not be disrupted quickly, either, when it does continue.[15]

Distractions, distaste, and other difficulties while praying are just so many human imperfections. But Augustine's emphasis on powerlessness and humility in God's presence does not mean giving in to pessimism. In a remarkable text, he says that our perfection as travellers en route resides in the effort to be aware of our imperfection. The perfection of travellers entails that they know that they have not yet reached their goal. "No matter how perfect we may be as human beings en route, we are well aware that we are not yet perfect". Our perfection in this life resides in the fact that we know that we are imperfect.[16] This is not said in order to make peace with all our imperfections, for we are able to grow toward perfection. Prayer plays an important role in this process. In a sermon, Augustine says to his listeners:

> "If my sermon has found in your hearts just a spark of such spontaneous love of God, nurse it carefully. Tell yourselves urgently to increase it by prayer, by humility, by the pain of repentance, by the

[14] Nat. et gr. 68,82. Perf. iust. 10,21.

[15] Ep. 130,10,20.

[16] S. Denis 18,3. Perf. iust. 8,19. S. 170,8,8.

love of justice, by good works, by sincere sighs, by a praiseworthy way of life, by loyal friendship".[17]

Precisely through the awareness of our imperfections, the child-like trust in God's accommodating love and grace blooms with splendor that is all the greater. God does not look so much toward the results of our efforts as toward the devotion of our will and our love.

"I think I can see that the psalmist described God as patient because he puts up with all the imperfections of our prayers and still waits hopefully for a prayer from us so that he may make us perfect...What are we to conclude? That there is no hope for the human race? And that if any thought sneaks into the mind of someone praying, and interrupts the prayer, that person is already fit for damnation? If we say that, sisters and brothers, I do not see what hope is left for us. Yet because there is hope for us in turning to God, because his mercy is great, let us say to him: Give delight to your servant; to you I have lifted up my soul, o Lord (Ps. 86:4)...You are kind, Lord, and patient; patient, because you go on tolerating me".[18]

In this text, our imperfections are approached from the perspective of the gracious God. But that does not at all mean that we, ourselves, need do nothing. We must, at least, regret our imperfections.

"We are bidden to ask that we may receive, to seek that we may find, and to knock that it may be opened unto us. Is not our prayer sometimes tepid or rather cold? Does it not sometimes cease altogether, so that we are not even grieved to notice this condition in us? For if we are grieved that it should be so, that is already a prayer".[19]

Quite in keeping with Augustine's description of prayer as longing, we ascertain once more that his response to the imperfections in prayer lies in the will or the desire to pray. If you want to pray, you have prayed.

[17] S. 178,10,11.
[18] En. Ps. 85,7.
[19] Simpl. 1, q. 2,21.

VIII. Christ and the Holy Spirit Praying in Us

1. Christ in Us, We in Christ

Augustine's conviction that Christ prays in us is based upon his idea that Christ and we, together, constitute the whole Christ. In doing so, he takes Paul's text as starting point: "In spite of the differences of its members, the human body forms one whole. All members, regardless of how many, together constitute one body. The Christ is so as well." (1 Corinthians 12:2). Christ is at the same time head and members. Head and members constitute one Christ. That is not because Christ would not be complete or perfect without us, but because Christ himself wishes to be one with us. Scripture teaches us that we can regard Christ in three ways: 1) as divine, equal to the eternal Father before he became human; 2) as God and human being simultaneously after he became human; 3) as the entire Christ, that is to say, head and body, according to Ephesians 4:13 "the perfect man, the entire scope of the fullness of Christ", in whom each of us is a member.[1] Augustine imagines the Christ's mystical union with us to be so great and so profound that he dares to say: "We did not only become Christians, we also became Christ... for the entire Christ is he and we".[2] Augustine bases his vision primarily upon two Scriptural texts: Matthew 25:40: "Whatever you have done for one of the least of mine you have done for me" and Acts 9:4 "Saul, Saul, why do you persecute me?" In modern spirituality, this idea of "the whole Christ" has been almost totally lost. And yet, this mode of seeing things is not so strange, if we consider that all love entails unification, identification but not identity. Out of love, human beings identify themselves with one another. In every love,

[1] S. 341, 1,1 and 9,11.

[2] Io. Ev. Tr. 21,8.

we see that human beings participate in each other's lives: in each other's thoughts, deeds, feelings, abilities, needs, faults, in short, in each other's good and bad points. We see this in the relationship between husband and wife, parents and children, friend and friend. This happens wherever true love is present.

The idea of the whole Christ is the basis for Augustine's texts concerning Christ who prays in us. The fact that Christ became human is the first foundation of his becoming one with us. It is his greatest deed of love. By assuming our human nature, he became one of us. From that moment, he also began praying as a human being.

"By the fact of being human, he was also weak, and in virtue of his weakness, he prayed...There you have both the majesty to which you pray, and the humanity that can pray for you...Why does he intercede for us? Because he consented to be our mediator".[3]

The fact that Christ became weak does not mean that he became sinful, but it does mean that he shares in the natural weakness of humanity in order to uplift it toward God. By becoming human, Christ encompasses all human beings. Out of love, Christ unites with both disbelievers and believers, and with the bad as well as the good. But there is a difference. Among those who do not respond to his love, the love comes unilaterally from Christ. Among those who do respond, it comes from both sides. Those who believe in Christ continue his life, which he lived here on earth in his human body. And so, there arises from the human being Jesus Christ, as the head, and from us, as his members, the new body of Christ, which is actually the continuation of the earthly body of Jesus. Christ lives and works further in this world in and through our physicality. He is still present here on earth to the extent that we are Christ's face and voice. We proclaim his message with our mouths; with our ears we listen to the needs of others, just as he did; like him, we have an eye for the poor and oppressed, and like him, we extend our hands to do good; like his

[3] En. 2 Ps. 29,1. En. Ps. 140,4.

in the past, our feet are directed toward the person toward whom no one goes. Where Paul especially uses the unity between Christ and us to show that we suffer in Christ, that we die, and are resurrected, Augustine will apply it to virtually all areas of life. Our sins are present in Christ because he takes them upon himself; our temptations are Christ's temptations; his anointing is our anointing; his words are in us, and ours are in him; our proclamation of the good news is his proclamation; our apostolate is his work; our sacrifice is his sacrifice; our sanctification is his sanctification.

The incarnation brought God and humanity together so that they became two in one flesh. "Two in one flesh" (Gen. 2:24) is the Biblical expression for the union of man and wife. Augustine applies it not only to the incarnation of the Son of God as such, but also to the unity between Christ and us as his body (see Ephesians 5:31). "If we confess that the head and the body are two in one flesh, then we must also recognize that head and body are present in one voice".[4] Another description of the assumption of human nature is "assuming the condition of a slave" (Phil. 2:7). Also on the basis of this text, Augustine arrives at the unity between Christ and us.

"Because Christ wished to assume the condition of a slave and within that condition to clothe us with himself, he did not disdain to take us up into himself and transfigure us into himself. He did not disdain to speak in our words, so that we in our turn might speak in his words... Were it not for the body's linkage with its head through the bond of love, so close a link that head and body speak as one, he could not have rebuked a certain persecutor from heaven with the question; Saul, Saul, why are you persecuting me? (Acts 9,4)".[5]

Augustine insists vehemently on our unity in Christ. By doing so, he does not shut out the Jewish people, and he freely cites Ephesians 2:14-16: Christ who made the two (peoples) one, in order to bring the two together in peace, to re-shape themselves to

[4] En. Ps. 40,1. En. Ps. 142,3.
[5] En. 2 Ps. 30, s.1,3.

a new human being and to unite both in one body for God. In this body, we are the children of God who call Abba, Father: Abba in the language of the Jewish people; Father in our language. The body of Christ is, in any case, not limited to a certain part of the earth any more than it is limited to a certain time. The body of Christ and the city of God have existed from the time of Abel, the first righteous person.[6] Thus, one human being, one unity of Christ comes into being. If we pray certain psalm words individually, it is one human being who does this, for we are all one in Christ. Every human being is one human being in Christ and the unity of the Christians is one human being. For this reason, Christ's voice is the voice of the whole world.[7] Our prayer is the prayer of the entire Christ, head and body, spread across the entire world. Because all are present in Christ's body, Christ speaks as one single human being. He, himself, is one person and many people. Viewed from the natural standpoint, we are many, but in Christ, we are one.

"O God, hear my prayer, give heed to my prayer (Ps. 61:2). Who is saying this? It sounds like a single person. But look at the next phrase, and you will see whether it can be only one. From the ends of the earth I have called to you, as my heart was frightened (Ps.62:3). So it cannot be one alone. Nevertheless it is one, because Christ is one, and all of us are his members. How can a single individual call from the ends of the earth? One person can, though, because what is shouting is the heritage promised to the Son...This possession of Christ, this heritage of Christ, this body of Christ, this one church of Christ, this unity that we are – this is what shouts from the ends of the earth".[8]

If we wish, we can all be the body of Christ. If we wish, we can be one, because the body of Christ is one. Each one of us has his or her share in the voice of the whole body. You have called in your days and your days have gone by. Someone else comes after you; he

[6] En. Ps. 78,3. En. 2 Ps. 90,1.

[7] En. 1 Ps. 70,6. En. Ps. 122,2. En. 2 Ps. 29,5.

[8] En. Ps. 60,2. En. Ps. 130,1.

calls in his days. You here, someone else there, and a third somewhere else. Every day, the whole body of Christ calls, while the members come and go. One person extends to the end of time.[9] This unity is obviously based upon love. Without love, it cannot exist. That applies to our love as well as to the love of Christ:

> "How, then, could these words of the psalm: Set a guard over my mouth, o Lord, that my heart may not turn aside, be correctly understood as spoken by Christ?... If these words are ours, how can Christ be speaking? If you ask that, I must ask you a question: Where is the love of which I was speaking a moment ago? Do you not understand that it is love that makes us one in Christ? Love cries out to Christ from our hearts, and love cries out from Christ on our behalf".[10]

Augustine presents the example of how our tongue shouts when someone treads on our foot or injures our hand. The tongue calls to protect the parts of the body: "you are hurting me".[11] It is the head's task to take care of the other parts of the body. By accepting a human body, Christ himself has willed to be our head. The caring love of Christ is clearly apparent from his identification with the poor and the persecuted. In their name, he says: "I was hungry and you fed me," (Matthew 25:35) and "Saul, Saul, why do you persecute me?" (Acts 9:4).[12]

On the basis of this inner identification, the voice of Christ and our voices have become one voice. It is this one voice that sounds in all psalms and prophets. In the psalms we find virtually nothing but the voices of Christ and his body, the church; and sometimes, the voice of Christ alone, sometimes that of the church alone – and we are that voice. When we recognize our words there, that does not occur without our being involved. We rejoice all the more if we feel we are present in it.[13] If the psalm beseech-

[9] En. Ps. 85,5. En. Ps. 83,5.

[10] En. Ps. 140,3-4.

[11] En. 2 Ps. 30, s. 1,3.

[12] En. Ps. 39,5.

[13] En. Ps. 59,1.

es, beseech; if it seeks, then seek; if it gives thanks full of joy, then rejoice; if it hopes, then hope; if it fears, then fear. Everything that is in the psalms is a mirror before us.[14] If the psalmist is in oppression, if he is worried, if he is sad, then we realize that we are in him, and we unite our prayer with his.[15]

"We should hear his voice in all the psalms, jubilating or groaning, rejoicing in hope or sighing with love in fulfillment. We should hear it as something already well-known to us, a voice most familiar because it is our own".[16]

But in the psalms, we pray not only with the psalmist, but simultaneously with Christ as well. This is even the case where it is a matter of liberation from sins. Even the call of Christ from the Cross: "God, my God, why have you forsaken me?" is cited by Augustine repeatedly. In such texts, Christ speaks in the name of his body, that is to say, in our name. He has taken over our voices as his own. But even in that case, one speaks of one single person because the head, Christ, never wants to be separated from us, his body.[17] In the case of the text "Lord, post a guard before my mouth and a closed door around my lips. Do not cause my heart to stray from the path toward malicious words to seek excuses for my sins" (Psalm 141:3-4), Augustine says that we may ascribe these words to Christ as having been spoken in our name:

> "Why do you pray in these terms, Lord? What sins have you, for which you would need to seek excuses? He will answer: When one of my members prays so, then I am praying so. Just as he told us: When you did that for even the least of those who are mine, you did it for me".[18]

Of course, we may not apply all Scriptural texts to Christ's identification with us. There are words in the Scripture that apply only to Christ alone, especially the texts that pertain to his divine

[14] En. 2 Ps. 30, s. 3,1.
[15] En. Ps. 54,5.
[16] En. Ps. 42,1.
[17] En. 2 Ps. 90,1. En. 2 Ps. 30, s. 1,11.
[18] En. Ps. 140,7.

exaltation, or his life's history. The text "They pierced my hands and feet" (Psalm 22:17) relates only to Christ's death on the Cross. Virgin birth, the fact that he is the Way, the Truth, and the Life, the fact that he is the only born Word of the Father pertain solely to him. At one time, Christ speaks in his own name, at another, in our name. He can say things without us, but we can say nothing without him.[19]

We must not regard this intimate, mystical unity of this mutual presence in each other as the language of imagery or something unreal. Augustine regards it as a profound reality. Do we not read in Galatians 2:20: "I live, but no longer myself; it is Christ who lives in me"? In this regard, Augustine points to the relationship between bridegroom and bride:

> "Christ is speaking here in the prophet. No, I would dare to go further and say simply: Christ is speaking. He is going to say certain things in this psalm that we might think inappropriate to Christ, to the excellent dignity of our head... and yet it is Christ who is speaking, because in the members of Christ there is Christ... He calls himself bridegroom and he calls himself bride (Is. 61:10). Why is he both bridegroom and bride, except because they will be two in one flesh? And if two in one flesh, why not two in one voice? Let Christ speak, then, because in Christ the church speaks, and in the church Christ speaks, and the body speaks in the head, and the head in the body".[20]

For this reason, we must not be afraid that our all too human, imperfect, and sometimes rebellious prayers would be unworthy of Christ. God could give us no greater gift than that his Word should become our head, a human among humans. Thus, let us not keep the Son of God separated from our prayers, but listen to the poor Christ in us and with us and for our sakes.[21] As our priest, he prays for us, as our head, he prays in us, as our God, we pray to him. There are many levels in our praying: praying to

[19] En. Ps. 142,3.
[20] En. 2 Ps. 30, s. 1,4.
[21] En. 1 Ps. 101,1-5.

Christ, praying in Christ, praying from Christ, praying through Christ, praying with Christ.

"When something is said about the Lord Jesus Christ, particularly in prophecy, which seems to imply some lowly condition unworthy of God, we must not shrink from ascribing it to him, who did not shrink from uniting himself to us… Yet then we hear him in some scriptural text apparently groaning; praying and confessing. We shrink from ascribing these words to him… Let no one, on hearing these words, maintain: This is not said by Christ, or, on the other hand: I am not speaking in this text. Rather let each of us who know ourselves to be within Christ's body, acknowledge both truths, that Christ speaks here and that I speak here. Say nothing apart from him, and He will not speak apart from you".[22]

Once again, love is the background of the unity between the praying Christ and us, because love never wants to be separated from the beloved. The love of Christ will never be unfaithful to us, who form his body. For this reason, the voice of the head never wants to be separated from the voice of the body.

"Since the whole Christ consists of the head and his body, we must be alert to the accents of the head in all the psalms in such a way that we catch the voices of the body too. He would not have us speaking apart from him, any more than he wants to be apart from us, for he said: Lo, I am with you even to the end of the ages (Mt. 28:20). If he is with us, he speaks in us, speaks about our concerns, and speaks through us, because we also speak in him".[23]

For us, this entails an important task as well. When we pray, we must not separate ourselves from Christ. When we hear his voice, we must not tear ourselves loose from his voice. For that reason, Augustine summons us to remain linked to Christ for all time through faith, hope, and love:

[22] En. Ps. 85,1.

[23] En. Ps. 56,1. En. Ps. 37,6.

> "Since the psalm sings to us of mercy and judgment, let us belong to the body of Christ, and we will sing Christ's mercy and judgment. Within Christ's body let us sing of these things. Christ is singing about them to us. If the head were singing alone, the song would be about the Lord but would not belong to us. But if Christ is a whole, head and body, you must be among his members and cleave to him by faith and hope and love. Then you are singing in him, and rejoicing in him, just as he labors in you, and thirsts in you, and hungers in you, and endures tribulations in you. He is still dying in you, as you have already risen in him... Let us then sing in hope, all of us, gathered into one.[24]

The last words of the text above clearly show that it is not merely a question of a personal, individual union with Christ. All other human beings are present in Christ as well because his love encompasses all. In him, we can feel at one with all people. For this reason, all are present in our prayers, and our voice expands to be the voice of all humanity. That applies not only to our prayers of petition, but to other forms of prayer as well. God also pays heed to the longing of the whole body of Christ, united in the one Christ, to see the Lord's salvation in the land of the living.[25] In addition to longing, we think here of praising God. Christ praises the Lord in the hearts of many. Because Christ praises God, Christians, too, must praise him. And if we praise God, then Christ praises him, because we are the members of Christ.[26]

To summarize, I believe that it is a great help, encouragement, and comfort for us that we must frequently regard our impoverished prayer as the continuation of Jesus' prayer in us. Even if we do not feel like it, or have difficulty praying, we know that it is our job to propagate the Lord's prayer further in the world. In addition, we know that we never pray alone, but that Christ prays in us, and also that through and in him, the entirety of humanity is present with us, at prayer. We can construe that presence in two ways, either in the sense that all the faithful pray with us, or in the

[24] En. Ps. 100,3.

[25] En. 2 Ps. 26,23.

[26] En. 2 Ps. 33,3. En. Ps. 108,32.

sense that we pray for the entirety of humanity. Thus, prayer always has a communal dimension.

2. The Holy Spirit in Us, We in the Holy Spirit

What is said regarding Christ's praying in us also applies to the Holy Spirit. Upon closer examination, in both cases, what we have is a union that comes about as a result of love. We offer our bodies to the Holy Spirit, because, as God, we owe him obedient service. For that reason, Paul says: "Glorify God in your bodies" (1 Corinthians 6:20).[27] The dwelling of the Holy Spirit in our hearts is, in the first place, the presence of divine love in us. The unity of the Spirit with us consists in the fact that the workings of the Spirit become our work, yet they remain a gift. The workings of the Spirit are more difficult to describe than the effect of Christ upon us, because on the basis of Christ's becoming human, his influence is more palpable, easier to grasp. The saving function of the Spirit has more a spiritual, inner nature. He causes God to be close to human beings and the world. He allows us to see God's love. He tries to win people for God, and, in the loving care of the Father, the Son, and the Spirit, he tries to bind the believer to God in a lasting way. The possession of God's Spirit means both invitation and grace.

We have already seen how the longing of many generations before us is present in our prayers. Augustine goes even further, however. In line with a tradition that goes back to Paul, he regularly emphasizes that it is the Holy Spirit that prays in us. The text that Augustine cites most frequently in his works is Romans 5:5: "For the love of God is poured out in our hearts by the Holy Spirit, which is given to us". If it is above all love that now prays – as we were frequently able to discern – then it will come to us as no surprise to hear that the Spirit prays in us. For the Spirit is the source of our love. It is the Spirit that causes us to love God:

[27] Trin. 1,6,13.

> "In order for you to love God, let God dwell in you, and love himself by means of you; that is, let him prompt you to love him, kindle you, enlighten you, rouse you".[28]

Through the Holy Spirit, not only do we call "Abba, Father" (Romans 8:15. Galatians 4:6), but "He comes to aid our weakness as well. For we do not even know what we should pray, but the Spirit itself pleads for us with unspeakable sighs" (Romans 8:26). Paul's comment about our ignorance with regard to our praying was, for the noble widow Proba, grounds to ask Augustine for an explanation. She must have thought: Is prayer such a puzzling activity that Paul can speak of ignorance here? Do we not find sufficient guidelines in the Holy Scriptures? Surely, Paul knew the Our Father? Initially, Augustine gives a rather short reply: "Insofar as the content of the prayer is concerned, I can sum that up as follows: Ask for a happy life in your prayers". Later in his reply, he penetrates Proba's difficulty more deeply. Especially in our misery, which can be both advantageous and disadvantageous for us, we do not know what we ought to ask. Paul was not heard when he asked to be saved from the thorn in his flesh so that he might not presume upon the exceptional revelations he had received (2 Corinthians 12: 7-10). Jesus prayed "Father, if it be possible, let this cup pass from me," but God wanted him to drink from it (Matthew 26:39). Whoever asks for eternal joy asks for the highest satisfaction and perfect peace. But, because it goes above all concepts, we do not know how to pray as it should be done. We ask for something we cannot conceive, which is tantamount to ignorance.

"There is in us a certain learned ignorance, if I may say so, but it is learned in the Spirit of God, who helps our infirmity... Therefore he makes the saints ask with unspeakable groanings, breathing into them the desire of this great thing, as yet unknown, which we await in patience".[29]

[28] S. 128,4.

[29] Ep. 130,4,9. 14,25-15,28.

According to this text, thus, there are two reasons for our ignorance. The first is that we do not know whether worldly goods are advantageous or disadvantageous. The effect of the Holy Spirit must teach us what serves the end of our salvation. Praying with sighs is the identifying characteristic of someone who is lacking something. But no one has understanding in the proper manner, no one has insight, excels in demeanor and strength, is consciously God-fearing, fears God in a pure way, if he has not received the Spirit of wisdom and insight, of demeanor and strength, of knowledge and fear of God, and of fear of the Lord (Isaiah 11:2-3). Without the Spirit of prayer, no one can pray for his or her salvation.[30] Already in one of his earliest works, Augustine declares that the Holy Spirit does not sigh as if he were in need or knew difficulties, but because he motivates us to prayer, and we do that under his influence, it is said that he sighs. Nor does he use the word "plead" there to describe the effect of the Spirit, but "urgently appealing".[31] According to Augustine, it is peculiar to a dove to sigh out of love. For that reason, in Romans 8:26, Paul uses the image of a dove in association with the sighs of the Spirit, as that occurs at several places in Scripture. But the holy Spirit does not sigh as a person of the divine Trinity. He sighs in us, that is to say: he causes us to sigh in prayer.

"The holy Spirit teaches us to sigh. He impresses upon us the fact that we are pilgrims; he teaches us to long for the fatherland. We sigh with this longing".

Augustine contrasts the sighing of a dove to the shrieks of a raven. The raven is, then, the image of human beings who are satisfied with worldly goods and look for nothing else. Augustine compares the shrieking of the raven with the many human beings who sigh under earthly misfortune, people who are crushed under injuries they have suffered, weighed down by physical illnesses, bound up in chains, cast about from side to side by the waves at sea, surrounded by the ambushes of their enemies, but they do

[30] Ep. 194,4,16-18.

[31] Gn. Adv. Man. 1,22,34.

not sigh out of love of God, nor are they driven by the Holy Spirit.[32] The Arians used the sighing of the Holy Spirit to deny the divinity of the Spirit. The Spirit who asks something of God cannot be God, for he who asks is sub-servient to him of whom he asks something. Augustine calls attention to the fact that "asking" is not the same as "adoring." The Holy Spirit does not adore the Father! For that reason, once again, Augustine gives a two-fold interpretation of the Spirit's continual pleas on our behalf. The Spirit does this because he is never absent from those who are continually driven to pray by a holy longing. For that reason, the Spirit pleas without interruption. Another interpretation points to the fact that the Spirit causes the saints to pray with sighs of holy longing. The God-fearing mind is a spiritual grace that is given to us by the Spirit. Whoever does not pray according to the inspiration of the Holy Spirit, prays only in accordance with worldly desires.[33]

The Holy Scriptures are inspired by the Holy Spirit. Prophets and psalmists were inspired by the Spirit. The Spirit had given them an ardent love of God. For us, this means that we must listen to them with the fire of the same Spirit. In this way, we hear the Spirit of God or of Christ in their words. Filled with the Spirit, they have praised God. And, because the Spirit of God praises him in his servants, God praises himself. [34]

"The Lord our God is here speaking to us in a comforting way, because he sees that by his just judgment it is only in the sweat of our brows that we eat our bread. And so he has deigned to speak to us from our own situation, to show us that he not only created us, but also dwells in us... With regard to the words of this psalm which we have just heard, and partly sung, we cannot say simply that they are our words... for they are more properly the words of the Spirit of God than our own. On the other hand, if we deny that they are ours, we are lying...The merciful Lord has deigned

[32] Io. Ev. Tr. 6,2.
[33] C. Max. 1,9. C. s. Arrian. 26,23.
[34] En. 1 Ps. 34,1. En. Ps. 144,1.

to speak to the miserable, and he deigns also to use the voice of the miserable. In this sense both statements are true: that it is our voice here and not our voice, that it is the voice of the Spirit of God and not his voice. It is the voice of the Spirit of God, because we would not be speaking these words if he did not inspire us... Our entitlement even to groan is the gift of God".[35]

In the Bible, the holy Spirit is frequently associated with heat and fire. These are, as it were, properties of the Spirit that is love. The heat is present in God's word. A fire burns in the heat of the word. The reality to which the word points is the glow of the Holy Spirit. In psalm 19:7, we read: "There is no one who can hide from its glow". And, in the case of Paul, we read: "Fiery through the Spirit" (Romans 2:11).[36] For this reason, the Holy Spirit, who is present in the prophets, gives us joy in the reading of their words. The Holy Spirit is also present in the psalmists. He inspired love of the city of God in the author of psalm 87. When he sings the praises of the holy city, we are made to listen, with the fire of the Holy Spirit, to what he has to say about this city.[37]

The fact that the Holy Spirit prays in us, and through him, we call "Abba, Father," are Augustine's most powerful arguments that prayer is a grace. We could add that faith in Jesus is also a gift from the Spirit, because "No one can say: Jesus is Lord, except through the Holy Spirit" (1 Corinthians 12:3). Particularly against the Pelagians, Augustine defends the view that praying is not something that we can ascribe solely to our own powers, but that asking, seeking, knocking are given to us. Calling to God with a heart that loves the truth and is in agreement with the Holy Spirit, is a holy gift. In addition, it is the Spirit that creates room in our hearts by giving us the fullness of dual love, both of God and of the people near us. For that reason, we must pray for the Spirit.

[35] En. 2 Ps. 26,1.
[36] S. 22,4,3. and 7,7.
[37] En. Ps. 96,1. En. Ps. 86,1.

"If you bad as you are, know how to give good gifts to your children, how much more will your heavenly Father give the good Spirit to those who ask him (Lk. 11:13). This is the Spirit through whom love is poured out in our hearts, so that by loving God and our neighbour we may carry out the divine commands. This is the Spirit in whom we cry: Abba, Father (Rom. 8:15). How can we be said to cry out if the Spirit himself is crying out in us? Surely because he has been making us cry out, since he began to dwell in us. Having received him, he works in us, empowering us to go on demanding more, so that by asking, seeking, knocking we may receive him in ever greater plenitude".[38]

Thus, we thirst for the good Spirit to do what we ourselves cannot do. But that does not at all mean that we must do nothing. It would be wrong to interpret the text of Matthew 10:20 "For it is not you who speak, but the Spirit of your Father speaks in you" as if we ourselves are excluded. Grace does not destroy human freedom. Prayer is no automatism, it requires our involvement. Thus prayer appears as a mysterious event between God and human being.

"It is not those impelled by their own spirit, but all those moved by the Spirit of God, who are children of God (Rom. 8:14). This does not mean they do nothing, but that they are moved by the good Spirit in the good deeds they do, for otherwise they might be active indeed but do nothing good. The more generously the good Spirit is bestowed on someone by the Father, the more she or he becomes a good daughter or son of God".[39]

In the Latin, instead of "doing" (active) and "being moved" (passive) the text says "working" (active) and "being worked" (passive): we work and are worked upon by the Holy Spirit. In this way, it is indicated that our working is dependent upon the involvement of the Spirit. Augustine formulates this thought as follows: "Someone says to me: We are thus worked upon; we, ourselves, do not work upon something in the world outside ourselves.

[38] En. 14,2 Ps. 118. Persev. 23,64.

[39] En. 27,4 Ps.118.

I reply: You, too, do something, but at the same time, you are worked upon. You do something good if you are affected by the good. Because the Spirit of God, who affects you, is for you who work, a helper. Even the name 'helper' prescribes that you, yourself, do something… Someone who does nothing, need not be helped".[40] In this text, we hear Augustine's doctrine on grace. We need divine grace to do good, but that does not suspend our free will and our involvement, or our responsibility. Even we have something to do. Prayer and grace go together. We never pray for anything within our power. No one asks for what he or she can do themselves. Thus, prayer shows our powerlessness. It is up to us to have the desire, but our free will must be goaded on; it must be healed in order to be able to act; space must be made in order to be able to receive; filling must take place in order for possession to occur. Prayer is necessary in order to accomplish what the law requires. In prayer, we recognize grace.[41] But there is even more. Prayer is not only a sign of the existence of grace, but it must, itself, be regarded as one of the gifts of grace. For that reason, Paul says: "We do not even know how we ought to pray. But the Holy Spirit expresses our plea with inexpressible sighs" (Romans 8:26).[42]

[40] S.156,11,11
[41] Gr. et lib. Arb.16,32. Bono vid. 17,21. S. fragment 4.
[42] Ep. 194,4,16-17.

IX. Method of Praying in Augustine

1. Ascension

Is there any such thing as a method for praying in Augustine? In the strict sense of the word, nowhere does he teach a method such as we find in the case of later spiritual leaders. Nor did he ever write a systematic book on praying. His concern had rather more to do with the creation of a spirit of prayer and a fundamental inspiration that makes prayer possible and accompanies it. This has the advantage that his ideas are quite supple and that they can be applied by anyone to personal circumstances and needs.

Augustine teaches a gradual growth in the spiritual life. Already in one of his earliest works, he describes four steps in our ascent to God. 1) Virtue: prayer supports the practice of moral virtues which mean a purification for us. Especially strength and moderation cause our benevolence toward others to grow. 2) Rest: rest consists, especially, in the establishment of our inner equilibrium to make the Christian ideal our own in faith, hope, and love. Prayer is the path to perfect justice and it provides the strength to continue. 3) Entering into the light: prayer leads us to contemplation of revealed truth. 4) Remaining in the light: here, our prayer is transformed into contemplation. Exultation and union with God are characteristics of this phase.[1]

Elsewhere, Augustine makes a combination of the beatitudes with the gifts of the Holy Spirit. 1) Poverty of spirit consists of humility and is in accord with fear of the Lord. 2) The meek who shall possess the Kingdom, live from the piety that is stored up with knowledge of the Scriptures. 3) Blessed are those who mourn, for they strive toward knowledge to know where they are still controlled by worldly goods. 4) Blessed are those who hunger and thirst for righteousness, in the quest of which, above all, they

[1] An. Quant. 33,73-76.

need strength. 5) Blessed are the merciful, for just as we need God's counsel and help, we must stand by the weaker with help and advice. 6) Blessed are the pure of heart, for they are the ones with a clear conscience to comprehend the greatest good. 7) Blessed are those who bring peace, for the contemplation of truth or wisdom brings the whole human being to peace.[2]

Thus, from Augustine's many texts concerning praying, we can derive a general line of thought. Praying is not an oppressive activity, but the breathing of our personal faith. It is our faith in action. The point of departure is God's presence within us. Praying is the affective elevation of the heart to God.[3] It is an ascent to God that is full of love. The word "affective" points to the fact that more is involved than an activity of the intellect. It has to do with the human heart and all the feelings that circulate within that heart. The word "exaltation" points to the fact that we must ascend above ourselves to meet God. Praying is a progressive motion toward God. In the ascent, we can discover a sort of "method". Augustine always begins by considering creation and reading the Scriptures (both the Old and the New Testaments). We can call this extensive instruction by creation and Scripture the given basis of prayer. Subsequently, Augustine sets out to apply the significance of the texts to himself. They are, as it were, a norm and a test for one's own life. For that reason, a person must enter within themself and allow his or her own heart to be influenced by what they have read.

2. Meditation

Allowing the word of the Scriptures to penetrate into ourselves occurs through meditation. Meditating is thinking about some-

[2] S. Dom. m. 1,3,10-4,11. Doctr. Chr. 2,7,9-11. S. 8,11,13. S. 347,2,2-3,3.

[3] F. Cayré, La méditation selon l'esprit de Saint Augustin. Paris 1934. S. Poque, L'expression de l'anabase plotinienne dans la prédication de Saint Augustin et ses sources, in: Recherches Augustiniennes 10(1975) 187-215 deals with the following texts: Conf. 7,17,23 and 9,10,24-25, S. 52,6,16-17, En. Ps. 41,7-8, Io. Ev. Tr. 20,11-13.

thing, considering something. Meditation is the consideration we find in someone who loves.[4] Among the monks in Augustine's time, meditation consisted either of singing and reciting psalms while at work and in the reading and study of the Scriptures.[5] Here it seems that study of the Bible or the content of our faith may be included in the concept of meditation. Above all, Christians must consider God's commandments. The goal of meditation is manifold. It can occur to impress a truth into the memory so as not to forget it, to deepen it and appropriate it, to absorb it into one's heart, so as not to have it heard only outwardly. Otherwise, the truth cannot become fertile. Meditating is thus an activity and an exercise. Meditation in rest must pass over into meditating in our actions. In the interpretation of psalm 63:7 "At daybreak I shall meditate concerning you", Augustine notes that we must not forget God when we rest; he must be present in our memories then as well. But here, daybreak signifies the beginning of our labors. If we are mindful of God when we rest, then we ought to meditate on him during our activities so as not to forget him in our labors. God must help us to do good works. But in the case of someone who does not think of God in his or her leisure and free time, how can that person think of God in his or her actions?[6] We can regard God's word as a seed that must bear fruit. For that reason, it is necessary to consider the word we have heard. It must strike our heart as if it were a plowed field. A farmer makes the hard clumps of earth fine so that the seed can penetrate it; otherwise, the birds will peck at the seeds. Something of that kind happens with meditation. But after that, God's rain must fall to make the planted ground fertile. God does this by visiting us at all possible moments: during our rest or activity, when we are in the house, or in bed, during a meal, a conversation, or a walk.[7] Thus, meditation is necessary in order to render God's

[4] En. Ps. 19,4 Ps. 118.
[5] Op. Mon. 17,20.
[6] En. Ps. 62,15.
[7] En. Ps. 84,15.

word fruitful. There are people who are eager to hear words of wisdom, but afterwards, do not reflect on them at all.

Augustine describes this meditation frequently, in terms that are quite concrete, with the expression "re-chewing," just as some animals re-chew their food to grind it finely, so that it can be absorbed more readily. Thus, it is also necessary to "re-chew God's word spiritually". In the Book of Proverbs 21:20, we read: "A treasure that is worth desiring rests in the mouth of the wise person, but the fool swallows it in one gulp".[8] The word of God, which we absorbed as sustenance, we must also "re-chew", otherwise the word lacks its effect. Listening to the word of God and not performing it means that we have not processed it properly.[9] The process of absorbing God's word occurs in four phases: listening attentively, storing it in the memory, re-chewing it by reflection, performing it by deeds.[10] Concerning his meeting with Ambrose, Augustine relates that he did not know what hope kept him going and inspired him, what struggle he had to withstand, what his comfort was, and what splendid joys the hidden mouth of his heart enjoyed in re-chewing God's bread.[11]

Augustine describes his own attitude as follows: "I meditate on the Lord's law, and though it may not be all night and all day, at least I do it at those times that it is possible for me to do so. And I set my reflections down in writing so that they do not escape through forgetfulness".[12] He also calls upon his faithful, not to forget the words of his sermons, but to continue to remember what they have heard from him, for example, by speaking with one another about it. Otherwise, his work would remain unfruitful for them.[13] God's word is food for us; it is bread for us. We live from it because it interprets the will of God, which must not leave our hearts. Therefore, we must eat the bread of the word day

[8] C. Faust. 6,7. En. Ps. 141,1.
[9] En. 1 Ps. 103,19.
[10] S. 228,2.
[11] Conf. 6,3,3.
[12] Trin. 1,3,5.
[13] En. 4 Ps. 103,19.

and night (cf. psalm 1:2). We eat it whenever we listen to it or read it. We re-chew it whenever we consider it to fix it in our memories. By considering it, we absorb it into our hearts.[14] This does not happen in order to lock God's word up in our hearts, but in order to touch God himself:

> "I have become aware that my God is some reality above the soul. I reflected on these things, and poured out my soul above myself (Ps. 42,5) that I may touch him. How could my soul ever attain what it seeks, the reality above the soul, unless it poured itself out above itself? If it remained within itself it would see nothing other than itself".[15]

Meditation leads to the awareness of God's grace. When the psalmist advises us to consider all of God's works, he impresses divine grace upon our hearts and he boasts of having found that grace, the grace through which we are redeemed gratis.[16] Thus, meditation has its own effects on the spirit, or affections. They arise especially if one looks at the world and observes the drama of nature, and if one seeks and finds therein the Artist, in whom we find more satisfaction than in all the rest.[17] Affection is part of love. Good meditation presupposes "belief that is effective through love" (Galatians 5:6), for without love, no one can reach eternal happiness. True meditation consists of reflection upon the law by someone who loves, and loves so strongly that the love of his reflection does not grow cool.[18] Finally, a meditation regarding present-day life is also oriented toward the future. The reflection must be rendered perfect in the praising of God, for therein lies our future life. The will to reflect upon our existence in this world should be present before eternal life dawns. Reflecting upon God's book is to reflect upon heaven.[19]

[14] En. 3 Ps. 36,5. En. Ps. 46 1.
[15] En. Ps. 41,8.
[16] En. Ps. 142,10.
[17] En. Ps. 76,14.
[18] En. 19,4 Ps. 118.
[19] En. Ps. 148,1. En. Ps. 93,6.

Meditation occurs in the human heart. There, people discover themselves and purify and re-shape their lives, both by fighting the evil within themselves, as well as by storing up the stock of virtues that direct them toward love of God and of their neighbors. "Descend; then you can ascend, and ascend to God".[20] The last phase toward which all the rest is aimed, is a certain union with God. The ultimate point of all prayer is to live with and in God. The union is a gift from God. Therefore, exulting in God's goodness and greatness is the apex of praying, as Augustine's *Confessions* clearly show.

The movement of prayer, thus takes on three principal phases: first, toward the external world, then from the external world to one's own heart, and then, from one's own heart to God. It is also possible to describe this process in other ways. Augustine wants to come from the many things that surround us and distract us, to the one that gathers and grants rest, he wants to proceed from the visible to the invisible, from the mutable to the lasting, from the transitory to the eternal, from the world to God. All these expressions describe what he means by "ascending". In order to be able to begin the ascension, human beings must be aware of the limitations of this world, with its suffering and death, anxiety and transitory nature. In addition, they must be aware of their own shortcomings and sinfulness. For this reason, no ascension is possible without humility. Humble persons direct themselves to God; self-satisfied persons think that they can do everything themselves and that they do not need God. There is no prayer without humility. Those who have delusions of grandeur can never sing "Praise the Lord, you children" (Psalm 113:1).[21] A person whose love remains limited to him- or herself and this world, leaves no place for love of God.

"If the soul remained within itself, it would see nothing other than itself. For there, above my soul, is the home of my God, there he dwells, from there he looks down upon me, from there

[20] Conf. 4,12,19.

[21] En. Ps. 112,1.

he created me, from there he governs me and takes thought for me, from there he arouses me, calls me, guides me and leads me on, and from there he will lead me to journey's end".[22]

It is precisely love that causes us to ascend to God. There is no other way. The steps to God are loving affects *(affectus)*. By loving, we ascend; by indifference, we fall down. While we remain on earth, we are in heaven, if we love God. The will to be lifted up to God springs up in our hearts. The movements of the heart are the internalized feet to move around, the stairs to ascend, the wings to fly.[23] When Augustine interprets the psalm verse "You have governed the ascent in the heart of the one who is supported by you" (Psalm 84:6), he says:

> "God sets up steps for him to climb. Where? In the person's heart. It follows then that the more you love, the higher you will climb… He can make no progress by himself, so your grace is needed to take him by the hand…Where are the ascents established? In his heart, in the valley of weeping… Let there be these steps set up by God through his grace. Climb them by loving. While you are climbing, the song of ascents rings out".[24]

3. From Meditation to Contemplation

Love is simply life that unites, or tries to unite, two things, namely the one who loves and what is loved. That is so even in the case of love of external and physical objects. If we want something more pure or more refined, then we must ascend to our spirit. But that is not enough, because from there, we must ascend even higher and seek that which is above us, to the extent it is given to humans to do so.[25] The words: "to the extent it is given to humans to do so" mean: to the extent that we are capable of

[22] En. Ps. 41,8.
[23] En. Ps. 85,6. En. Ps. 38,2.
[24] En. Ps. 83,10.
[25] Trin. 8,10,14.

doing so, to the extent that our powers suffice. Augustine is convinced not only of the fact that to this end we need the grace of God and the help of Christ, but also that God, in his infinity, remains superior to us. By longing we ascend, and as we ascend, we sing the stairway song, in which we say: "I have raised my eyes to you, who dwells in heaven" (Psalm 123:1). Ascending from earth to heaven is a difficult task. Even if we take heaven to mean the vault of heaven that we see with our eyes, then there are such great distances and an immeasurably great separation! In addition, we see no stairway with our eyes extending from earth to heaven. Are we wrong, then, when we sing the song of ascents? And yet, we do ascend to heaven when we think of God. He gave us the power to ascend in our hearts. Ascending in our hearts is making progress upon the pathway to God. To do that, we must not place ourselves at the center of our thoughts, but rather, we must direct our spiritual gaze toward God. But even then, we do not see God face to face, because we are still living by the faith, and we continue to see as in a foggy mirror. For that reason, Augustine gives a symbolic explanation of the word "heaven": heaven is all the holy and righteous souls, in whom God dwells. If our ascent consists of love, then heaven consists of righteousness.[26] God is nearby, yet far away. The God in us is the God above us.[27] God and heavenly joy are, at the present time, still unimaginable.

"Now as I said: We will contemplate God, you cried out in longing for a beauty not seen as yet. Let your heart stretch beyond all familiar things, let its gaze beyond all the things you are accustomed to think about which are derived from the flesh, all the thoughts drawn out from the fleshly senses and any kind of fantasies. Drive the whole lot out of your mind. Whatever presents itself to your thoughts, turn it down. Recognize the weakness of your heart, and whatever occurs to you, say of it: That is not the real thing, for if it had been, I could not even have imagined it".[28]

[26] En. Ps. 122,3-4.
[27] En. Ps. 130,12.
[28] En. 2 Ps. 26,8.

According to Augustine, not only is God unspeakable, but also incomprehensible, or rather: because he is incomprehensible, he is unspeakable. God surpasses our ability to comprehend. We can touch God with our spirit, with the purified eye of our heart, not with our understanding. The light that we touch is unfathomable. We can never com-prehend God:

> "Is anyone able to conceive in his heart or embrace with his mind how good the Lord is? But let us turn our gaze back upon ourselves, recognize him in our own being, and praise the artist in his works, because we lack the capacity to contemplate him in himself. One day, perhaps, we shall be able to contemplate him, when our hearts have been so purified by faith, that they can at last rejoice in the truth. But now, while we cannot see him, let us gaze upon his works, so that we may not fall silent in our praise".[29]

For that reason, our contemplation here in this life is always imperfect. Perfect contemplation of God is reserved to the eternal life. Our souls are now too weak, because they are so changeable and limited. Our souls now take one step backward, then they make progress again; now they know something, then again, they are ignorant; now they remember something, then they forget something; now they want something, then they do not want it; now they are righteous, then they sin again. And yet, our "incipient contemplation" on earth, as Augustine calls it[30], is not insignificant. With our spirit we touch God, if only a little. Even if we contemplate God, just to a slight degree, it is the approach and gives a foretaste of satisfaction. Our longing to experience God's presence now will one day be satisfied. There is thus no disruption between earthly and heavenly contemplation.

Augustine knows three ways of Christian life: the active, the contemplative, and a mixture of both. The truth is needed for both action and contemplation, but contemplation, in particular inclines toward looking at the truth. And yet, he finds that no

[29] En. Ps. 134,5.

[30] Io. Ev. Tr. 124,5.

one may be so absorbed in contemplation that the contemplative gives no thought to the benefit of others, and conversely: the active person cannot be so caught up in activity that he or she neglects the contemplation of God. Contemplation consists of investigating and discovering the truth, but of doing it in such a way that the fruits of contemplation are not withheld from others.[31] Augustine reports how people who are exhausted by the hectic world come to seek rest among contemplatives. They seek rest with them in God's word, in their prayers, psalms, hymns, and songs. The monks listen to them, comfort them, give them courage, and point out their faults. Should we fail to do this, they say, we would be dealing with God's spiritual food in a dangerous way.[32] The proper pathway through life may be found in both contemplation and activity: namely, keep directing one's gaze toward the Lord. Rachel, Mary, and John are, for Augustine, models of living contemplatively: Lia, Martha, and Peter, of living actively.[33] Taking action for the sake of earthly things, without which this life cannot be lived, in an intelligent way, pertains to the active life; for this reason, we must do that under the accompaniment of contemplation of the eternal goods that we must acquire.[34] Augustine refuses to regard the contemplative life as inactivity, for it too entails an aspect of activity. The activity consists of praying, fasting, giving alms, subduing destructive habits, and bearing with one another in love.[35]

Contemplation is fixing the gaze of the soul upon God, with awe and respect. But even within contemplation, Augustine draws a distinction between our contemplation now, in this life, and later, in eternity. Our lives are lived out in faith, while the life to come will be lived in the vision of God. Along the

[31] Civ. 8,4. 19,1-2 and 19.
[32] Op. mon. 1,2.
[33] C. Faust. 22,52-58. S. 104. Io. Ev. Tr. 124,5-7.
[34] Trin. 12,13,21.
[35] Ep. 48.

pathway of faith, we must come to looking face to face. Even the least sophisticated among the faithful, those who have no notion of invisibility, immutability, or lack of physical presence, are to reach that goal through the crucified Christ. And yet, faith, as incipient contemplation, sheds some light upon, and provides a certain experience of God's presence.[36] Now there is the light of faith and the light of hope.[37] Our likeness to God must grow, and it grows the more we love. Then we approach God, and we experience God more profoundly, because God is love. At the same time, we experience something that we expressed in words and were unable to express in words. Before the experience, we thought we could express God in words, but now we learn that we cannot say what we are experiencing.[38]

"After all, the name Israel is translated as one who sees God. I beg you, pardon me, if you do not want to be Israel. I want to be Israel. I want to be counted among those who are permitted to see God. We thank him who makes us to see now in a mirror and in a dark manner, but then face to face, as the apostle says (1 Cor. 13:12). We see by his gift, even when we still see in a mirror in a dark manner, we see nevertheless, how these two things are not contradictory: that the Father and the Son and the holy Spirit are distinct and that these three together are still one Lord God... Believe and you will see it".[39]

Even the name "Zion" is connected to contemplation in this present-day life in faith. Zion is the city of God and it means "the looking," that is to say, vision and contemplation. It is having a view of something, looking somewhere, directing the gaze of the spirit toward something in the distance so as to see it. Thus, every soul is Zion when it strains to see the light that must be seen.[40] Contemplation of God is the highest virtue. Caution, modera-

[36] Io. Ev. Tr. 124,5-7. Ep. 120,1,4.
[37] En. Ps. 37,15.
[38] En. Ps. 99,5-6.
[39] C. Max. 26.
[40] En. Ps. 98,4.

tion, righteousness, and strength are virtues for this life, but the contemplation of God has eternal value because "the God of gods will appear in Zion" (Psalm 84:8).[41] A condition for receiving the inner light is that our eyes be pure and simple. By believing, and loving one's neighbor, we purify our eyes in order to be capable of seeing God, for in love we see God to the extent that this is possible on earth. We carry our neighbor and go toward God. But we do not yet see him, toward whom we are progressing. We do believe in him.[42] Another condition is rest and tranquility. In tranquility, the truth that is within us speaks. Of those who lead a life of rest, the church says: "I sleep, but my heart is awake" (Song of Songs 5:2). This amounts to the following: I rest so that I listen. Whenever the human spirit finds rest after hectic activities, it expands with divine motions of the spirit. A certain solitude of concentration *(solitudo intentionis)* is necessary because reflection requires separation.[43]

Only after this life will nothing prevent us from looking at God as he is. Then we shall see him face to face (1 Corinthians 13:12). But at this moment, we are preparing ourselves for the inexpressible sight, or, as Augustine formulates it:[44] for the invisible vision. Now that we must still rely on faith, the promise of the vision, itself gives us joy; but how much greater will the joy be when the promise is fulfilled and God gives himself to us. In this regard, Augustine appeals not only to Paul's opposition of the dark mirror and seeing clearly face to face, but also to 1 John 3:2 "Beloved, we are already the children of God, and what we shall be is not yet revealed. But we know that when it is revealed, we shall be like him, because we shall see him as he is". Our resemblance to God will be perfect only as our vision of God is perfect.[45]

[41] En. Ps. 83,11.
[42] S. Dom. m. 2,22,76. Io. Ev. Tr. 17,8 and 11.
[43] Io. Ev. Tr. 57,3 and 17,11.
[44] Io. Ev. Tr. 53,12.
[45] En. Ps. 75,5. Io. Ev. Tr. 3,17-18 and 53,12. C. Max. 2,26,12. Trin. 14,17,23.

4. Ecstasy

And yet Augustine believes that a few privileged souls have seen God's being here on earth. That applies especially to Moses and Paul, the two leading guides persons insofar as the revelation of God is concerned: Moses for the Old Testament, Paul for the New. In ecstasy, both saw God as he is. Augustine knows two sorts of ecstasy or spiritual rapture: a natural one, which can be caused, for example, by anxiety or panic, and one that is given by God, which is based upon grace. The latter is a subject of importance for us. If the soul ascends above itself toward God, it is drawn away from the physical senses and carried off to God. It is alienated from the world and is, as it were, dead with respect to life here, for no one can see God and remain alive (Exodus 33:20). This alienation from the world is described by Augustine as "a holy or sober inebriation", having been made drunk by the Holy Spirit, drunk due to the abundance of God's house (Psalm 36:9). That is human language for the purpose of expressing the divine.[46]

The Bishop of Hippo wrestled with the opposing statements that "No one has ever seen God" (John 1:18) and the many appearances of God that are related in the Bible (appearances to Abraham, Isaac, Jacob, Moses, Isaiah, Micah, Job, Paul). He interprets most of the appearances in the sense that God availed himself of an earthly form, or an angelic figure in order to appear. God spoke to Moses through a cloud on Mount Sinai, an angel in the tent of the revelation, and a fire in the burning bramble bush. And yet, Augustine acknowledges that Moses had direct contact with God on the basis of Numbers 12:6-8: "To your prophets, I reveal myself in visions and I speak to them in dreams. With my servant Moses, I do not do that. He is my confidant… I speak to him, from one mouth to the other in a direct vision, and not in riddles. He beholds the glory of the Lord:". Paul had the same sort of direct contact with God: "Must he be praised, though

[46] S. 34,1,2. S. 225,4,4. En. Ps. 35,14-15. En. Ps. 74,12. C. Faust. 12,42.

there is nothing to be gained by it? But now I come to visions and revelations of the Lord. I know a human being in Christ, who was taken away fourteen years ago, in the body or outside it, I do not know, God knows – the person was snatched away to the third heaven… and he heard unutterable words that no human being is capable of saying" (2 Corinthians 12:1-4).[47]

And yet, there are a number of texts in Augustine in which he stresses that God appeared to Moses in some sort of material shape, and not in his own being, because this is reserved to the saints in the other life.[48] And frequently he cites the words of Paul, that only later shall we see God face to face. How are these texts to be brought into line with Augustine's conviction that Moses and Paul certainly saw God's being? I believe that Augustine's texts themselves contain the answer. The particular texts he is interpreting must be borne in mind. And as we said, he assumes that there are only two texts that speak, unambiguously of seeing God directly, namely Numbers 12:6-8 and 2 Corinthians 12:1-4, though he leaves the possibility of such a vision open for other "spiritualized" people.[49] With respect to Moses, Augustine notes that God can, at the same time, appear and remain hidden, or better: He appears as the hidden one. Seeing something is, in any case, something different from comprehending something in its entirety as a result of having seen it, so that nothing remains hidden. We cannot see the fullness of the Godhead (Ephesians 3:19).[50] What applies to Moses applies to Paul as well: Paul saw what God is, in himself, but with this reservation "to the extent that the human spirit, which is not what God is, could comprehend a little, though that be ever so slight, and only after the spirit was purified from every earthly stain and alienated and removed from all physicality and material likeness". God is Light itself.

[47] Gn. Litt. 12,26,53-28,56. Ep. 147,6,17-13,32.

[48] En. Ps. 43,5. En. Ps. 138,8. Io. Ev. Tr. 3,17. Io. Ev. Tr. 53,12. Civ. 22,29. C. Max. 2,25,10.

[49] Io. Ev. tr. 98,8.

[50] S. 23,14,14. Ep. 147,9,21.

Human beings are not sufficiently powerful to reach that light completely, and they shake out of weakness.[51] To the extent that Paul could, he dwelt with his heart in "unspeakable contemplation". When Paul says that he heard unutterable words, then this shows sufficiently well how unutterable God is![52] Even for those who can touch God, it remains impossible to comprehend him. They see and experience, as it were, God's incomprehensibility.[53]

If we turn to Augustine himself, we can ask the question whether he included himself among those who had achieved this climax of contemplation. He does confess that he is not able to direct his spiritual gaze toward God's goodness as it is in itself, but that he does believe in the possibility that there are human beings with stronger spiritual sight than his, who can concentrate the attention of their hearts on what God is in himself.[54] But, on the other hand, he admits: "I myself have sought my God, not only to believe, but also to see something of God, if I could". And he adds: sometimes we comprehend something of God's house; we touch that which extends above our souls; we can see something unalterable, though only in passing and for periods of short duration.[55] In this life, we can touch God only for periods of brief duration. It is a contact and a transitory touching, as Augustine has splendidly described in his *Confessions.* In the account that has been called "the ecstasy of Ostia", he describes how he had a conversation with his mother, Monnica (shortly before her death), in which they wondered what eternal life would be, a life that no eye has seen, no ear has heard, and has not appeared in any human heart. Their heart's mouth longed for water from the wellspring of life, which is God. To the extent that they were able, they wanted to be sprinkled with it and, in one way or another, comprehend something of such a

[51] Gn. Litt. 12,28,56 and 31,59.
[52] En. Ps. 119,2. S. 117,5,7.
[53] S. 117,3,5.
[54] En. Ps. 134,6.
[55] En. Ps. 41,7-10.

great reality. After having come to the conclusion that sensual pleasures are not comparable to the joy of the other life, he continues:

> "Then we oriented ourselves with an even more ardent emotion to him, who is always the same. By degrees, we went through all material things, and heaven itself, where the sun, the moon, and the stars cause their light to shine upon the earth. And, thinking, and talking, and admiring your works, we ascended within ourselves. We reached our minds and climbed out above them, to reach the region of inexpressible superfluity, where you pasture Israël eternally, with the truth for food. It is there that life is wisdom through whom all present things come to exist and even those things that were, and those that yet shall be. But the wisdom itself is not created, but is as it always was, as it always shall be… And while we chatted and longed for it, we touched it with all the exertion of our hearts. We heaved a sigh… and turned back toward the noise of our mouths, where the word knows a beginning and an end".

What is noteworthy in this text is the transitory nature of the high point of contemplation. The exalted contemplation ends with a return to the common word that we say every day. For that reason, Augustine and his mother Monnica go further with a contemplation of the "great silence" of all created things as a precondition for seeing and hearing God himself.

"If the tumult of the flesh fell silent, and silent too were the phantasms of earth, sea and air, silent the heavens, and the very soul silent to itself, that it might pass beyond itself by not thinking of its own being; if dreams and revelations known through its imagination were silent, if every tongue, and every sign, and whatever is subject to transience were wholly stilled…: if God alone were to speak not through things that are made, but of himself, that we might hear his Word not through fleshly tongue nor angel's voice, nor thundercloud (like the law given at the Sinai, Ex. 19) nor any riddling parable, hear him unmediated, whom we love in all these things, hear him without them, then it would be as now that my mother and I stretched out and in a flash of thought touch that eternal wisdom who abides above all things. If this could last, and all other visions, so far inferior, be taken away, and this sight alone ravish him who saw it, and engulf him and hide him away, kept for inward joys, so that this moment of knowledge – this passing moment that left us aching for more – should there be life eternal, would not 'Enter into the joy of your Lord' be this, and this alone? And when, when will this be? When we all rise again, but not all are changed".[56]

Some have levelled the charge at Augustine that in his efforts to ascend to God, he neglects the world. But is it possible to think of God's transcendence if one does not ascend beyond the world? Augustine wishes to stress, in strong terms, in addition to God's residing within us, God's exaltation above everything that is created. As I see it, this is entirely in keeping with the faith of the Bible. Turning inwards to ourselves certainly does not mean leaving creation. We need our bodies. Knowledge of the meaning of created things can be considered as referring to the Creator. By means of visible things, we try to ascend to the invisible God by leaving the visible world temporarily. In addition, we must not forget that Augustine, too, is ordered to go back from the top of the ascent down to daily life. When he interprets the text: "In my ecstasy, I said: I am banished from your sight" (Psalm 31:23), then he points out that we can, indeed, have a spiritual contact with God, but that God remains unfathomable, and our weakness is not capable of maintaining that contact fully for long. We are referred by God back toward humankind.[57] "Being referred back to humankind" is the opposite of an unearthly existence. Augustine does not regard the ultimate term of the vision of God in individual terms, but as a charismatic function in the service of the people of God. Even if, for a moment, the ecstasy ascends above the earth, its fruits are entirely earthly. They may be found in the spiritual energy for everyday life: in joy, peace, reconciliation, trust, patience, optimism, and above all, in the love of one's

[56] Conf. 9,10,24-25. See A. Mandouze, Saint Augustin. L'aventure de la Raison et de la Grâce. Paris 1968, 666-714.

[57] S. 52,6,16.

neighbor. Augustine's aim was to ascend to God by way of the world, by way of the body, by way of the senses, by way of the memory, to esteem them according to their own rank and value:

"This is what I do often and is my constant delight, namely ascension to God. In such meditation I take refuge from the demands of necessary business, insofar I can free myself. Nowhere amid all these things which I survey under your guidance do I find a safe haven for my soul except in you. Only there are the scattered elements of my being collected, so that no part of me may escape from you. From time to time you lead me to an inward experience quite unlike any other, a sweetness beyond understanding. If ever it is brought to fullness in me my life will not be what it is now, though what it will be I cannot tell. But I am dragged down again by my weight, sucked back in everyday things and held fast in them".[58]

Augustine comforts himself with the thought that one day, it will all be different.

"After this age God will rest, as on the seventh day, when he will cause the seventh day, that is us, to rest in God himself...This seventh day will be our sabbath, and its end will not be an evening, but the Lord's day, an eighth eternal day, sanctified by the resurrection of Christ, which prefigures the eternal rest of both spirit and body. There shall we rest and see, shall see and love, shall love and praise. Behold what shall be in the end without end".[59]

A total love of God that surpasses all other longings, a continual unification with him, a profound inner joy, boldness in prayer combined with great humility, is that not enough to call Augustine a master of prayer? For him, prayer is not an exceptional moment in the life of a Christian, but an intimate union of the soul with God. However, the union must also be expressed in deeds.[60]

[58] Conf. 10,40,65.

[59] Civ. 22,30,5. Cf. En. Ps. 85,24.

[60] M. Vincent, Saint Augustin, maître de prière, d'après les Enarrationes in psalmos. Paris 1990, 451-452.

INDEX OF SCRIPTURAL TEXTS

INDEX OF THEMES AND NAMES

PRINTED ON PERMANENT PAPER • IMPRIME SUR PAPIER PERMANENT • GEDRUKT OP DUURZAAM PAPIER - ISO 9706

N.V. PEETERS S.A., WAROTSTRAAT 50, B-3020 HERENT